UNSHACKLED
AN AUTOBIOGRAPHY

HORACE LEON IVEY SR.

ISBN 979-8-89112-608-4 (Paperback)
ISBN 979-8-89112-609-1 (Digital)

Covenant Books
11661 Hwy 707
Murrells Inlet, SC 29576
www.covenantbooks.com

To my wife, friend, and companion, Felicia Gaskin-Ivey, for supporting me through this journey.

In loving memory of my sister, Iris "Nene" Denise Ivey (January 12, 1960–February 5, 2022). I will always love you and miss you.

This book is dedicated to my mom, Thelma Ivey (November 4, 1923–January 21, 2021). Thanks, Mom.

Contents

CHAPTER 1

REAL LIFE STORIES

As Jack lay dying, he said to Charlie, "She did this to us," meaning their mother's lifestyle, the life she lived in front of them. Billy and I don't talk as much as we used to, but I still remember the times when we would talk about our childhood experiences. He remembered once when his father hit his mother in the eye, recalling the redness because she was a bright-skinned woman. The anger of seeing that still haunts him to this day. An auntie of mine is still traumatized from the abuse she suffered from my uncle for almost forty-two years of marriage, abuse he suffered from his father. That is the family that my mother grew up in most of her young adult life.

I had a neighbor who was from an Asian country who told me about her mother and siblings being physically abused by her father in that country. It's not just physical abuse. The mental state is probably the worst. Some physical wounds heal, but mental abuse can last a lifetime.

I talked to people all of the time, and I lived in several states, cities, and towns. People from every walk of life, young and old, of different races are still traumatized by mental abuse. I have siblings who have lived in abusive relationships for years, thinking that it's normal. From childhood, I have seen continued abuse from men that my mother allowed to come into our home. Although they did not live there, the pain of watching my mother being pulled by her hair still brings back those hurtful emotions. I lived with that from the age of eight years old.

We were children being exposed to adult situations. I sucked my fingers as a child up until I was about twelve or thirteen years old. I would always be thinking about my mom and what effect it would have on me if she passed away. I would ask God, "Please don't let my mom die before I do." Well, God answered my prayer. Mom lived to be ninety-seven years old. After becoming a Christian, I stopped being afraid of Mom dying before me.

I began praying that she would become a Christian. All throughout my childhood, there were oftentimes just fear, uncertainty, and disappointments. It seemed as if Mom couldn't live without a man in her life; most of them were married men. This created fear in my life—just the thought of Mom being caught by one of their wives.

Back in the '60s, when I was around six or seven years old, Mom was messing around with this piece of a man—yes, married. He only had one eye. I remember his wife coming to our house with the police. Imagine what effect that had on me and my siblings. I just stood there with my fingers in my mouth and wondered what it was all about.

My sister was about one year and a half younger than I. She had to have been exposed to some of the same mental abuses. There were eight children born into this situation, ranging in age from one year old to twenty years old. My oldest sister, who is twenty years older than my younger brother, talks often about the challenges she had to face during the years of my momma's childbearing. My mom was born into a fairly large family herself—ten. She almost always talked about her childhood, about how she had an abusive, angry father; again, I was a child listening to an adult talk about physical and mental abuse. In the '60s, the singer Dionne Warwick recorded a song with the line "What's it all about, Alfie?" ("Alfie"). And that is how my life would be for most of my adult life, wondering what it's all about.

When it came to discipline, that meant whippings. Mom would wait for things to build up within herself. In anger, she would beat us for the old and new. Mom would beat me with whatever she could get her hands on, even extension cords. We called them drop cords, growing up.

Chapter 2

CHILD ABUSE

I didn't know then that it was really child abuse, as I know it to be today. That saying goes, "Spare the rod, spoil the child." There were no spoiled children in our household, although my younger sister and brother may not have gotten as many beatings. Mental illness can be brought on early in life. In fact, I started suffering mental illness in regard to physical abuse when I was only a young boy.

We grew up in poverty, so I know a little something about not having enough food and clothing. There were times when Mom would move from one house to another, a rental property. When we got home from school, we would have to find out where Mom had moved. Talk about confusion. Wow!

There were many negative influences in my growing-up stages, mainly from Mom and my eldest siblings. They were the people I spent most of the time with.

I can remember as far back as possibly four to five years old, maybe even younger. I was very inquisitive when I was a young boy. When things were happening within the home, I was curious about what I observed, say like Mom's having this one-eyed man staying overnight in her bed. Most of what I remember are actual events in my personal experiences. When I talk with my siblings, they would tell me about their experiences with Mom and within our home.

Being the middle child, I grew up with all seven siblings—two brothers and five sisters. In our early lives, there wasn't too much to laugh and tease about; just surviving and getting through the day was challenging enough, such as a lack of food, electricity, etc.

Some of my early childhood memories of mental abuse started when I was about four or five years old, when I saw my mother's sister actually slap my mom in the face, as if Mom was a child. This particular sister was younger than Mom was. It scared me so badly, but I could only look on with fear and with my fingers in my mouth. I wonder why my auntie was attacking my mom. This happened in the Mosquito Bottom, a community that I grew up in as a child.

We moved several times during my childhood, so I can remember things that happened in my life. Long before I started school, I had, at the time, two younger sisters, whom I, at times, had to babysit. Imagine a five-year-old boy babysitting a three-year-old and a one-year-old child. We lived on Norris Avenue. My older brother and sisters were in school, so when they were gone out of the house, I had to be home with my young siblings at five years old. I didn't always make good decisions, really!

On Norris Avenue, I can remember when we hardly ever had enough food to eat. Looking back, I ask the Lord, "How did we survive?"

Mom worked domestically out of the home, so she would be what they called at that time working on the Lot. She lived with the woman she worked for, cooking, cleaning, and raising her two sons. In retrospect, Mom lived better than we did. I never thought about that until in recent years.

We were children raising children. There were many devilish things to get into. One of my older sisters who is six and a half years older than me used to love watching soap operas at twelve years old. What did she learn from those filthy shows? Filth.

Let me say this: being ignorant about your past is one thing, but being stupid is totally another. I found that if you have been in prison and can help or stop someone else, tell your story. God can use you to help others. Don't be afraid or ashamed to let the world know that you are free at last. Thank God I am free at last (John 8:32 NKJV).

Being a child should be the best times of our lives. Unfortunately, because of parents who don't know any better, we suffer many kinds of abuses. Growing up, there was a plethora of neighbors who were just plain ignorant when it came to raising children. I believe that had my mom known better, she would have done better. As the saying goes, "Ignorance is not bliss, it's a disaster" (Thomas Gray, eighteenth-century poet).

Do you know the phrase "ignorance is bliss"? It means that if you don't know about something, you don't need to worry about it, or you can essentially ignore it. Being in a state of ignorance deprives your chance of taking any actions that could ultimately produce the results that you have always wanted. In other words, ignorance holds you back from what you want to achieve by limiting your belief.

Now let me say this: Don't get me wrong, there were good influences in my life as well. Mom taught me the value of hard work, respect for my elders, how to laugh and poke fun at my siblings, and others. She endeavored, at times, to point me to God, the little that she knew about him.

I can look back and remember as a young boy, the earliest influences in my life were my older brother and my next older sister because they were whom I was around most of the time as a child. We lived in close-knit communities back in the day, but I wasn't exposed to the neighbors as much as I was my older siblings. Like I said earlier, I learned most of my habits from the elder brood.

I always call myself a mama's boy, meaning I wanted to be around my mom as much as possible. Mom epitomized what I thought, as a child, the meaning of what a mother should be. She never, at that time in my life, told me that she loved me, but somehow, I knew she did. Mom worked hard to provide food and housing for her children, but most of the time, that was about as far as that went. As children, we often went without some of the bare necessities of life—clothing, shoes, food, etc. We made do with what we had handed down or given to us.

I've always been fascinated by people from large families. I guess growing up, we didn't have toys or much of anything. We played with each other. There were also many close relatives to be around with.

My aunt, who had a large brood of children, had an impact on my childhood as well. Looking back from as early as five or six years old, family were my biggest influences. It wasn't until I started school that the neighborhood began to help shape who I was to become.

My prayer for this book is to give my children's children and the generations after them clarity into their family's history, things that will help them to avoid ancestral pitfalls that so many families experience through not knowing their history, pitfalls such as possibly getting involved with affairs with relatives, going through multiple divorces, having children out of wedlock, mental illness, living in poverty, and not knowing the God of their fathers.

One good thing about having older siblings is that they help fill in some of the blank spaces in your memory, like remembering you or reminding you about the different places that we lived, and we did live in several rental houses in Charlotte. By the time I started first grade, we had moved a multitude of times. Though, as told by my eldest sister, I was born on Shannon Street, right off Independence Boulevard. Our back door actually faced Independence Boulevard, in the community known at the time as Brooklyn.

Now, from birth to about four or five years old, we had moved to North Norris Avenue. This is where I really remembered some of my first experiences of being aware of my surroundings and sibling experiences. I hadn't started school yet, so I would babysit my two younger sisters. It wasn't by choice. It was what families did, sometimes children raising children. Today, this would be called child neglect.

I can remember my next eldest sister coming home from school or sometimes not going to school. At those times, I loved being with her. My earliest time of being exposed to soap operas came from me watching them for hours at a time with her. I grew up watching *As the World Turns*, *Guiding Light*, *General Hospital*, and later on, *All My Children*. Imagine what I was learning at such an early age.

My older siblings attended Druid Hills Elementary School. Back in those days, I would be so happy when they came home from school. At that stage and time of my life, I wasn't introduced to academia, such as reading, writing, and arithmetic. All that I learned primarily was passed down from Mom, my siblings, television, and cartoons.

From Norris Avenue, we moved across town to Alexander Street, right next to the railroad tracks. This is where I began to grow and start venturing out. We moved into a house right beside my eldest sister, her husband, and their children. Alexander Street was where I began to grow interested in reading, since I never saw or remember seeing any books in the home. We would occasionally have a newspaper in the house, The *Charlotte News*. I believe this is where I began wanting to learn how to read. I would take whatever paper it was and go down the pages, underlining or circling the word *the*. Hey, it was a start!

As a child, all I wanted to do was play. I hung around with my older brother most of the time. He was about five years older than me. I adored my brothers and sisters. At that time, my younger brother hadn't been born yet. As a matter of fact, I never knew that Mom was pregnant with him. In those days, that wasn't something that children would know about. I know now it takes at least nine months for a baby to be born. But as a seven-year-old child, I thought, *Where did he come from?* My mom wasn't in the home most of the time, so we watched each other.

CHAPTER 3

MOM WASN'T THERE

Mom worked for a white woman named Ms. Condrick. For many years, in fact, she helped raise her two sons. Mom lived at Ms. Condrick's home most of the time. Therefore, I only saw her periodically. I would be so happy when Mom was home. I loved Mom.

Mom worked seemingly all of the time. There were holidays when we would have just each other to be with. My siblings and I were very close-knit back then. I began to venture out more and more on Alexander Street. We had neighbors who lived next door to my eldest sister. We had neighbors who lived behind us. We lived across the street from a mattress factory. On the left side of our house were the railroad tracks. As I remember now, we had lived on the other side of the tracks when I was about four or five years old at 923 North Meyer Street.

At Alexander Street, that was when I would experience the beginning of some of my most traumatic abuses, psychologically speaking. Neglect is the most common form of abuse or child abuse, followed by physical abuse, sexual abuse, and psychological abuse. We would experience not having food to eat a lot of the time. Like I mentioned before, Mom worked away from home, spending many days and nights away from us. We were children raising ourselves. At seven years old, I was exposed to probably all of the aforementioned abuses. Because these are my life experiences, I will endeavor not to call any names.

At seven years old, I hadn't yet started any kind of schooling, reading, writing, and arithmetic. What I was learning was poverty, sex, sometimes mental and physical abuse. From the older siblings, because Mom was a single parent, it seemed as if she attracted the wrong kind of men, mostly married men. I remember once when one of her men was at our home in the late hours of the night, one of the wives brought the police to our house to fetch her no-good husband. There was all this noise at the front door, this stranger and police talking to my mom through the screen. I stood next to Mom, wondering with my fingers in my mouth, *What's this all about, Alfie!*

There was a time when I was lying on the bed when all of a sudden, one of my siblings came into the room, picked me up, and placed me belly down on a hot woodstove. I still have a scar or two. I had family who lived not too far from us. Three of my older siblings actually witnessed a murder. They shared it with me when they returned to the house. Talking about fear, this fear lasted long into my teenage years.

Even to this day, when I hear about all these dysfunctional families, blended families, single parents, and yes, families with two parents in the home, I think of how there are still all these abuses happening right within the homes. It's critical that parents understand that they can expose their children to demonic activity from an early age, which can affect them for the rest of their life.

Jesus asked the parents of the little boy, "How long has this been going on in your son's life?"

They answered, "From childhood."

Again, there at the house on Alexander Street, which I mentioned earlier, was where I also was exposed to, what is called today, homosexual activity. At seven years old, I began to hang out with boys who were five and six years older than me because there were no responsible adults around. These older boys, including relatives, were experimenting with each other, and for a brief moment, they involved me. Thanks be to God—whom I didn't know at the time—he didn't allow me to be damaged mentally.

All of this was happening to me when I should have been in school. Parents should never, if possible, allow their young children, boy or girl, to hang around older siblings or relatives or friends. I have had friends who are now adults tell me how that they were sexually abused by an older relative. To this day, they are still in bondage to that assault.

Alexander Street was where I also started school. I didn't start school until I was seven. I was behind in learning just the basics—reading, writing, and arithmetic. The year I started first grade, which would have been September of 1965, I was not prepared. Mom hadn't gotten any of my documents together, such as my shots, birth certificate, etc. Up until about fifth or sixth grade, I went by the name Horace Vinson.

Mom later explained what happened with the name-change situation. She had a cousin whose name was Vinson. He and his wife had sort of raised me for a brief period. That is where the last name came to be. Well, for some reason, the day that I started school, and I will never forget, I was out in our yard at Alexander Street, playing with no shoes on, dirty clothing, not prepared for going into a school building. A cousin of mine, who was about three or four years older than me, came by our house that day, asking why I wasn't in school at this time of day. He decided to take me to school just the way that I was dressed—no shoes on, dirty clothing, and no legal documents. That's how I started Alexander Street School back in the fall of 1965.

At that time, Alexander Street School was totally a black school. Man, can you imagine as a seven-year-old boy what was going on in my mind? My cousin just dropped me off in one of the first-grade classes and left me there. I didn't understand what had just happened. Oh, yeah, Alexander Street School was across the railroad tracks, within walking distance. This was probably the most traumatic time that I had ever faced up until this point in my childhood. You ask, "Horace, where was the adult supervision at this point in your life?"

Like I said earlier, we were children raising ourselves. Mom was working on the Lot, as it was called then. I can only imagine what my younger sisters were doing at that time. I can only imagine—ignorance, poverty, no foundation, structure, or discipline. We cannot leave children exposed to these kinds of abuses.

CHAPTER 4

PEOPLE ARE TALKING

Over the many years since I began telling my story, I sat and talked to literally hundreds of people who have shared some of the same experiences as I have, but in different, manifold ways. Some of those same people were either denying or too ashamed to open up about the hurt and embarrassment.

As I remember, my first-grade teacher was a beautiful bright-skinned woman named Ms. Martin, a seemingly very gentle and polite woman. I don't remember attending school on a regular basis. We were poor and, a lot of times, couldn't afford the clothes, shoes, or just the basic necessities of life. Just getting food for the day was challenging enough. Even at that time, free meals were available, breakfast and lunch. I don't remember learning much in first grade, but I was finally exposed to reading, writing, and arithmetic. I was eager to learn, but I was so far behind. As you may imagine, that first year was very challenging. I was in and out of school and always struggling to survive.

Remember, I had younger and older siblings experiencing the same things, even to this day. When we get together, we share our past hurts. Thank God for his indescribable love. Well, if you can imagine not being in school more times than attending school, I failed the first grade. At the end of the school year, probably June, the practice at Alexander School was they would call out the names of children who had been promoted, and the remainder of those who had failed first grade would line up and be taken to next year's classroom. That way, you would know your teacher for the upcoming school year. As we entered the new teacher's classroom right away, I knew that it was going to be a long summer. My new teacher's name was Ms. Brenda, a bright-skinned woman also, but stern and very strict, unlike Ms. Martin.

Having failed the first grade, that allowed my younger sister Nene to catch up to me, so we ended up in the first grade together. I remember my little sister being so gregarious, energetic, and full of life when she had entered first grade at Alexander Street School.

As I sat here writing, I think about my little sister, being so bubbly at six and a half years old. So full of life, Nene passed away February 5, 2022, at the age of sixty-two. I believe that this is catharsis for me. This word derives from the word *cathartic*, meaning providing psychological relief through the open expression of strong emotions, causing catharsis. Crying is a cathartic release—purging, cleansing, releasing, relieving, delivering, and freeing.

The second go-round in the first grade was probably the same, except now I had a little sister to look out for and protect. Going to school did allow me to meet friends who lived in the surrounding neighborhoods. Heretofore, I only played with my siblings and nearby relatives. Now, I was exposed to other families who seemed to be not so dysfunctional.

Well, another year passed, and I was promoted to second grade at Alexander Street School. My teacher was Ms. McComb. She was a jet-black woman and just as stern as Ms. Brenda was. We moved from Alexander Street to Belmont Avenue when I was in second grade. I don't remember much about my second grade, except that after being in school for almost three years now, I was learning to read, write, and do arithmetic. On Belmont Avenue, I was maturing from being exposed to new friends. Now in a new neighborhood, there was growth taking place in my personal life. Nonetheless, the poverty still existed. Even to this day, when I see children who come from single-mother homes similar to where I came from, I endeavor to reach out as much as the situation will permit.

On Belmont Avenue, there were five of us living in a one-bedroom duplex. I don't, to this day, know what Mom was thinking. One bathroom? Come on, Mom.

My older brother and my next older sister didn't live with us much at Belmont Avenue. Wherever they were, I missed them fiercely. Holidays were especially hard on me. I just couldn't understand why we didn't have new clothing on Easter or toys on Christmas. I would see other children in the neighborhood dressed on Easter Sunday. We would spend the whole day in the house on Easter. Just didn't want to endure the shame nor the poverty. Wow, being poor is no joke.

One important thing that I do remember about our stay on Belmont Avenue is that we had food—yes, food. Evidently, Mom, in all her wisdom, decided to get the government-supplied food, pork and gravy, cheese, yellow grits, Spam, the big blocks of pure butter, oatmeal, powdered eggs, powdered milk, syrup, and flour. I believe, hey, it was a step up.

After living on Belmont Avenue for seemingly a short stay, we moved to North Harrill Street, a couple of blocks from where we lived. What is so memorable about the move from Belmont to Harrill Street? One day when my brother and I came home from school, Mom had moved, and we didn't know where she moved to. You talk about trauma, confusion, neglect, abuse, abandonment— all of the above. If only we could have known a little about child psychiatry, mental illness, emotional disturbance, and abnormal behavior—what?

Our move to North Harrill Street wasn't any better than the other places we lived. As a matter of fact, it was worse—right beside the railroad tracks *again*. This house was rat infested and had its share of roaches. The house wasn't well insulated. We heated the house with a wood stove. The wind would come through the windows. You talk about psychological warfare. Even as a boy, I knew this wasn't normal. There had to be something better.

At North Harrill Street, I don't remember attending school too often. We were still going to Alexander Street School, where I was in second grade. I did make friends at school and began to develop social skills. With all of the moving, lack of the bare necessities of life, and failing first grade, I began to act out my anger toward Mom and my peers. All of the years of abuse began to play out in my everyday choices. I even became promiscuous at an early age.

We finally transferred from Alexander Street School to Villa Heights Elementary when I was promoted to third grade. Society called it "social promotion."

While living on North Harrill Street, I begin to venture out more. It seemed at this time, Mom was home more. My older brother and sister were around the house more. Again, the closeness of my siblings was always, in my opinion, where my security and confidence were developed. As you may notice, I haven't mentioned much about God.

CHAPTER 5

FAMILY AND FRIENDS

On North Harrill Street, there were a multiplicity of families living up the street from us. Our house faced Lowders Fuel and Coal Company. Again, we lived on the left side of the railroad tracks that I mentioned, as well as the rats and roaches. Oh, yeah, I did.

At this time, Mom had started working at Southeastern Chicken Poultry, a chicken processing plant located on Central Avenue. Well, when Mom worked there, our menu at home changed somewhat. Instead of government-supplied food as our staple meals, we now enjoyed the luxury o—yes, you are right—chicken. Mom worked at the poultry for many years. However long she worked there, we ate chicken every day. Mom prepared chicken all kinds of ways. I was even introduced to boiled chicken feet.

I have always enjoyed the closeness of my seven siblings. Yes, there was dysfunction, but as a child, you don't understand what these abnormal behaviors are. We played just like the other neighborhood children. Some of them had mothers and fathers living in the home, and they were as messed up as we were—in other words, dysfunctional.

There was this one family. I will just call them the Smiths. Man, they had a father who was afraid of his wife. The wife was so jealous of him. At times, she would physically attack him. They had about ten children, as I can remember. Five or six of them were boys. When I wasn't home or at school, I would be at the Smiths' house. There

15

were families all over the place, and I didn't mind meeting new ones all of the time.

My eldest sister had long before gotten married and had her own family, but she always was there for Mom and her younger brothers and sisters. She would visit us on a regular basis, being married and raising her own children. She didn't know some or most of what we had to be exposed to.

Although Mom was working a stable job at the poultry and was at home in the evenings now, all the years of neglect—children raising children—had now began to surface. I never liked being in the house, so I would find any neighborhood boy who would venture out with me. Just a sidenote, I don't understand how young boys today can be around the house and say that they are bored.

We lived close enough to the train tracks to throw a rock, and most of the time, that is what we were doing, throwing rocks. I remember the first time that I got into trouble with the police was when I was about nine years old. Nothing serious, some of my neighborhood friends and I had climbed on a boxcar that was parked on the railroad tracks full of rocks. Well, we had a field day just throwing rocks everywhere. Unknown to us, throwing rocks at city vehicles even though they were parked in the city parking lot was illegal! Someone had called the police and reported our mischievous activities.

As the police arrived, they were standing at the bottom of the boxcar, beckoning for us to come down. One by one, we climbed down the ladder attached to the train. Man, can you imagine the fear that I felt back in the late '60s? The police would take young juveniles to the jailhouse and talk to them about more serious crimes that happened throughout the city. They would show us guns and other weapons people used to do crimes.

Well, after all the things to keep us from coming back, they had to call our parents. I would rather they locked me up even though I was just nine years old, as opposed to Thelma Ivey coming to uptown Charlotte to the Charlotte Police Department. On top of that, she had to walk. My Lord! One wouldn't walk side by side with Mom when she was mad. If you did, she would show you how mad she was by hitting you on your shoulder blade, so I walked fast in front of her.

I have many fun memories there at Harrill Street. There were other times that weren't so enjoyable. I mentioned earlier that among the eight of us, there were four daddies. Well, Mom held on to the worst one. That was the man whose wife had brought the police to our house a few years back. I don't mean to offend anyone, but I have to tell my story. On top of all the other abuses that I witnessed, now this little piece of a man who had only one eye—God forgive me—would come from his home to mess around with my mother and, at times, would physically abuse Mom in front of her young children. He had no respect for himself, Mom, or her children.

One Friday night, this sorry piece of a man—I don't apologize for the verbiage—took my mom by her hair and literally pulled her out of our front door. I can remember standing there, feeling so help-less with my two fingers in my mouth. The scene has played back in my memory for years. Talk about mental illness, anger, etc.

We walked several blocks to get to Villa Heights Elementary, meaning my little sister and I. She was in third grade also. There were other children walking to school from Harrill Street also, so we played all the way there. I had made several friends while living in the close-knit community.

Now Mom had begun seeing another man. He was married also. Mama, mama, mama. One thing about Mom was this: she wasn't gay! She loved men, and she was not interested in messing around with another woman.

Although this man was married and took care of his own home and was just as filthy as the one-eyed man, this man helped us to move to better and bigger housing. Now we were moving from North Harrill Street to Parkwood Avenue. This move would bring us closer to our new school and also to meet new friends. Like usual, we stayed in contact with our old friends for a while, and then we would move on to other friendships.

CHAPTER 6

MOVING ON UP

The move to Parkwood Avenue was a move upward like in *The Jeffersons*. We had moved to a somewhat better living environment. The house was bigger and more suitable for six children. For the first time in our lives, we had our own beds. The bathroom was in the house instead of on the back porch. We even had gas heat. Yes, no more using wood and coal.

As we settled in on Parkwood Avenue, things were better as far as housing, food, etc. But Mom's choice of men continued to haunt me or us. The one-eyed man continued to surface from time to time. Now the new man was coming around. This created fear amongst me and my siblings, never knowing what was going to happen to Mom when these two married men would meet at our house at the same time. The weekends were the most traumatic times. This was when the men would show up the most—the alcohol, sex, and the like.

Nevertheless, life went on. We were at Villa Heights Elementary School now. I was in third grade. My teacher's name was Ms. McMichael. She was somewhat a motherly woman but tough. I began to enjoy school now more than ever. I wanted to learn reading, writing, and arithmetic. I started applying myself more in the classroom. My challenge was after school, I wanted to be out playing. Homework was not something that I welcomed or enjoyed. I had formed new friendships in the class as well as in the neighborhood. Life was good—family, friends, and school. Let me say this (and all due respect to Mom): I think I had the greatest mom in the world. She loved the heck out of her children, figuratively speaking. She did the best that she knew how. I believe that had she known better characterwise, she would have done better. I loved my mom. I adored her. She wasn't a bad mother. She just made bad choices when it came to choosing her men.

Now we were in our new school, a better living environment, a new neighborhood, so to speak. Just because we moved into a better environment, it didn't lessen the psychological abuse; the physical and verbal abuse still affected my mental and emotional well-being.

At Villa Heights Elementary School, I began to grow and mature more. Being at school around my peers challenged me to learn academically. While in Ms. McMichael's class, I met another boy who had stayed behind many years in school. His name was Paul. He and I became childhood friends in the classroom and after school. Paul lived several blocks down Harrill Street, so after school, I would go down to his house. We would hang out and talk for hours at a time. He lived with his grandmother, brothers, sister, and many other relatives—and that same house, dysfunctional.

As a third grader at Villa Heights Elementary, I loved physical education, music class, and most of all, lunch. Back in those days, if we couldn't afford lunch, I lived close enough that I could go home on my lunch period. We had to get permission from our parents.

My little sister Nene, who had caught up with me in first grade, was now in third grade with me. Her classroom was next door to mine. Ms. Newberry was her teacher. We shared a lot of time together also, but at that time, she had begun to get her own friends. Nene was very smart and sociable, always meeting new girls to play with. She loved going to school.

Back in those days, children would have fights in school and finish them after school. We fought, made up by the next day, and became even better friends. Nene had a mean streak and would fight boys as well as girls. She was my sister. Many times, I would have to step in when someone whom she had started trouble with wanted to get revenge on her but was bigger than her. You just didn't mess with my sister.

We had moved to Parkwood Avenue, but I didn't right away begin to venture out into the neighborhood for probably another year. Well, another year passed by, and I was promoted to fourth grade—social promotion. My fourth-grade teacher was Mr. Jensen. At Alexander Street School, there were only black teachers. Villa Heights Elementary School had become desegregated by then, and I had my first white teacher, Mr. Rudd Jensen. He was a short, fat man who walked tall and carried a large stick. You talk about strict. Wow!

Although the class was mixed with black and white students, Mr. Jenson didn't seem to be racist, a word I wasn't acquainted with back then. Mr. Jenson would carry a tablet with him at all times. As we went to the restroom, lunch, music, and physical education, he would be writing down our names in this tablet of those of us who would be talking too much, getting out of line, and just being children. We couldn't talk at the lunchroom table. Wow! Well, about the end of the day, according to how many checks you had by your name, that is how many paddles or licks you would receive. Forgive me for my verbiage again, but this fat white man could whip some *butt*. He would call our names one by one, black or white. He had to have another teacher present as witness. He did not spare the rod.

As I've mentioned before, my little sister Nene, who had caught up with me in first grade, was in a class next door. On Fridays, Mr. Jensen and Ms. Lofton, I believe that was her name, would bring the two classrooms together and would have a spelling bee. We would make a circle around the room, and the teacher would give the word to be spelled. I would be one of the first to sit down. Nene would pick at me for days. I loved my sister.

Another year would pass. Now, I'm in fifth grade, and my teacher's name was James Hagen. He had been in a serious accident that summer before school and was always in pain. He was a mean man and hardly ever had anything good to say about me. That school year, I'd missed a ton of days out of school, and when I did come to Mr. Hagen's class, he would say, "Until you can come to school for a whole week, you are not part of my classroom." He would sometimes send me to the neighborhood store to purchase him cigarettes and say, "Keep the change." Hey, it worked for me.

My last year at Villa Heights was probably my best year that I ever enjoyed. I was in sixth grade now and was coming to school more. I was learning more academically, participating in intramural sports within the school, and getting to know the white kids who were bussed from other neighborhoods. I started playing Pop Warner football between the ages of ten and twelve years old, and I was excited about playing in junior high.

My sixth-grade teacher was Mr. Greer. He was a bright-skinned black man, tall with salt-and-pepper hair. He was stern and strict but was fair. Talk about discipline, he was no nonsense.

As I look back, those men teachers really helped keep me in line, so to speak. As children, we need male role models, men who are decent and care about our well-being.

School, sports, and growing up on Parkwood Avenue helped shape me into a strong preteenager. I was growing stronger physically as well.

Home life was good most of the time at this point in my life. We had the sibling rivalries, etc. My older brother, who would go over the top at times, could be physically abusive.

With all the good things going on the outside of my life, the years of the neglect, poverty, filth, psychological abuse, and the ungodly lifestyle that I had witnessed up until this time; the memory of seeing my Mom physically abused by that one-eyed married man; the embarrassment and shame were always haunting me. I even talked to grown men and women who are still confronted with the same experiences as I did because of the lack of parental guidance or influence.

No matter what we call success in this world, if we don't deal with our past trauma, no amount of money, jobs, houses, cars, women, men, jewelry, art, or academic degrees can satisfy what our longing soul is crying out for—peace. God is the only one, through his Son, who can satisfy a sin-sick soul. I will get back to this subject later in my story!

Well, it finally happened. Sixth grade was over now. Another year had passed by with so many good memories.

I was thirteen years old now and had gotten promoted to the seventh grade in Eastwood Junior High School. My best friend at that time was Thomas Fleming. He would always be telling me about Eastway and what new white friends he had made. He would talk about how much he enjoyed going to school. Tom and I probably became good friends that summer before I entered seventh grade. Tom came from a big family like mine. There were ten of them. I also became good friends with Thomas's brother Willie. I started hanging out with the Flemings more and more. They become my second family. I simply adored the whole family.

The summer before Eastway, I had spent most of the time spending the night at the Flemings' house. I enjoyed both Tom and Willie. My Mom thought that the Fleming family was a good influence on me and didn't mind my spending time with them. I was getting to know them. They were also becoming acquainted with my family. Tom's mother—who was a tough, stern little woman— always welcomed me into their home. I was there a lot of times. Tom's father, Mr. Clarence, didn't say much about my visiting, and most of the time, he would come to the door when I visited.

Tom and I would do some silly stuff, just being teenagers. Willie, who was maybe a year older than Tom and me, played around with us sometimes but was more serious and more mature than us. Hanging out with my second family was really helping shape my life as a teenager and getting me prepared for junior high school. Up until then, I was so immature.

The reason I'm sharing this is because of the great impact that being around the Fleming family influenced my life so much. I'm so much of who I am today because they welcomed me into their lives.

Sometimes, if not most, having a father in the home has a great impact on the children. The father may not be all that, but he makes a world of a difference.

I didn't like being at home that much because of the environment at times. Mom was a single woman and liked her men sometimes too much. At this time, there were two married men in her life.

One of them was still—yes, you guessed it—the one-eyed man. Not knowing when these two men would meet up at our house, although neither one of them stayed with us, caused fear in my sister and me.

Mom worked Monday through Friday and, most days, would come home and cook. She did the motherly duties. Mom was a hard worker, and most of her children learned our work ethics from her, except one!

Moving to Parkwood Avenue was the beginning of a lifelong experience and the making of many friendships. I was growing up mentally as well as physically. I had become sexually active at an early age, so you can only imagine what was on my immature mind—sex.

Being around some of my older siblings at so early an age, watching them indulge in sex-related activities only broadened my curiosity about sex. Mom didn't make it any easier for me either, being that she would have men staying overnight at our home and yes, sometimes hearing and sometimes walking in on the very act of her sexual activities.

This kind of exposure for a young boy or girl has a profound effect on young children. It causes scars that can and will last for a lifetime. Little that I knew, many of the other children in the surrounding neighborhoods were experiencing some of the same sadistic trauma.

It's sad to admit that so many children were and are still plagued and exposed to this kind of lifestyle. And I hate to say it, but they will continue to be exposed to this lifestyle as long as parents and adults don't wake up and realize that children will grow up too.

Seeing Mom or hearing Mom having sex with different men caused me to become very angry and promiscuous. I had a love-hate for Mom. On one hand, I loved her because she was my mother, and on the other hand, she just didn't seem to care about her children regarding her sexual indulgence. So growing up, my personality and character were shaped and developed on these premises.

That summer, before entering the seventh grade—and I'm not proud of it, but it's true—I had multiple sexual relationships with some of the neighborhood girls. I hope that those adult women will get my book, read it, and understand where I started this lifestyle. I ask for your forgiveness.

CHAPTER 7

MY JUNIOR HIGH YEARS AT EASTWAY

Well, Eastway, here I come! Summer was ending, and I was in seventh grade now. I have finally caught up with my age group. Tom was in eighth grade now. We rode the same bus to school. Parkwood Avenue, Harrill Street, Allen Street, Davidson Street, and Pegram Street—the whole neighborhood was bursting out with children, preteens, as well as teenagers. Some of the older teens had moved on to high school. Parkwood Avenue was filled with families from one end to the other. Most of the children came from single-parent homes.

Nevertheless, here I go—the first day of school, dressed up. It was customary back then, and even now, to go to school prepared with paper, notebooks, pencils, pens, etc. I will never forget the excitement and the anticipation and joy of going to Eastway Junior High, the Trojans!

Entering Eastwood Junior High, for me, was like entering into another world. It seemed as if the whole world had suddenly opened up. New friends, new school—just simply a new life, so to speak. My seventh-grade teacher was Mr. Bridges. He was kind of a chubby white man, soft spoken and easygoing. He was my homeroom teacher. Going into junior high, we changed classes throughout the day. I think we had about seven classes. Some of my Villa Heights classmates were in the same class with me.

Eastway was where I began to excel academically. I've always wanted to learn, so here is my chance to catch up intellectually and socially with the older teenagers. There were so many opportunities for me—sports, student council, etc. I was somewhat popular in my neighborhood, and that reputation followed me to school.

In Mr. Bridges's homeroom, the class would vote on who they wanted to represent them on the student council. Well, because of the reputation I had with my peers, they voted for me in on about everything. Just a little sidenote: you never know what influence you have on other people, so be careful how you live your life before them. It can be good, or it can be bad.

My little sister and I started school at Eastway Junior High; we began associating with black as well as white children. Nene and I loved to be around other teenagers. We didn't spend much time together at this juncture, but she was still my little sister, and I was responsible for her as her big brother. Looking back to those earlier days from 1965 to the early '70s, I realized that my sister had experienced some of the same physical, physiological, sociological, and parental neglect as I did, if not more. I was growing up myself and didn't know much about the different stages of life, early adolescence generally, ages eleven to fourteen, middle adolescence ages fifteen to seventeen, and late adolescence ages eighteen to twenty-one.

At thirteen years old, I was totally ignorant and, to tell the truth, unprepared for all these seemingly sudden changes. And there were the girls—yes, girls—everywhere. I heard someone say if a boy became what he thought about for the first twenty-one years of his life, he would become a girl. Just kidding!

All throughout my childhood, I was confronted with promiscuity, the fact or state of being promiscuous. This led me to become even more sexually active in junior high school. I had been exposed to this kind of lifestyle as a very young boy. It was like a possession.

When I started attending Eastway Junior High in the early '70s, there were black teachers who cared about their students. This one teacher, who was my guidance teacher, was a sophisticated and astute lady. Ms. Robinson said to me one day, "Horace, if you want to go anywhere in life, you will have to work on your vocabulary. In other words, you better learn how to talk grammatically relating to conversation." From that day even to now, I work on speaking and improving my repertoire.

In my younger years, because of the immaturity, I was often hardheaded. I would have to go around the same mountain several times before I got it. That cost me most of my young adult life.

Eastway would become a refuge for me. I loved going to school. This was the first time ever that I spent more time in school than at home. All my friends were there, going to different classes, sharing lockers with classmates, walking up and down the many hallways. The freedom of being in junior high was awesome.

I didn't play football in my first year, but I was studying and carrying my books home from school. This was something new. Nene and I were so excited about school. Nene was smart and could learn easily, but I had to work at learning. My sister was very athletic also.

This is my story, so I'll include my sister at times, as I was recalling some of the notable events that happened the first year at Eastway. I had an opportunity to talk with one of Nene's close friends who also lived in our neighborhood. She reminded me of some of my devilish ways, not that I didn't remember. It's amazing how people can remember your *dirt* and not theirs.

Well, one morning coming to school on the school bus, all of the bus riders would gather in the hallways just talking and playing around before the bell rang, before we had to go to our homeroom. This particular morning, and I'll never forget, I ran into a student who happened to be white. Remember, race relations were still something we had to deal with.

Well, as it happened, I got into a fight with this white kid. I was already mean as Hades and could hold my own in fighting. When growing up in a large family, you had better learn how to protect yourself. Well, I picked this kid up and body-slammed him on the concrete floor. Before I realized what had happened, this kid was seriously hurt. I didn't wait around to see what was wrong. I hurried to Mr. Bridges's class I was in shock, not knowing what I had done, so I sat there in my seat, just confused.

About or within fifteen minutes, Mr. Bridges called my name and asked me to accompany him to the office. Mr. Miller was the principal at that time. He was a good man, Nevertheless, he had to suspend me until further notice. Because race relations were already at an all-time high, there were tensions flaring all over the school. I was sent home and had to deal with Mom. I explained to Mom what happened, but she was also concerned about the student.

For the first time in my teenage life, I had to go to juvenile court. This incident was sort of a prelude to other offenses to come, little did I know.

Mom had to take time out of work to accompany me. She did not like or couldn't afford to miss work. I missed school tremendously. After attending juvenile court and being slapped on the wrist, I was allowed back in school. I got over the incident and moved on. I would see the kid from time to time and wanted to tell him that I was sorry but never got up enough nerve to do so.

I returned back to school and was more determined to stay out of trouble as much as possible. As a teenager with so much unharnessed energy, I just wanted to enjoy being at school and around my peers. School was a safe haven for me, so to speak. One of my many enjoyments at school was lunchtime, being in the commons area. Eastway had a jukebox, and many of us seventh graders would gather around and listen to our favorite music. Some of us would even dance. One of my favorite childhood friends who knew how to do the robot very well would entertain us for a minute or two. Man, we had fun.

Sometimes just for entertainment and sheer ignorance and attention, I would get a group of boys and clog up the entranceway to the commons area, knowing that this would cause racial tension and confusion. Yes, it was fun at the time. I enjoyed going to class when I wasn't doing something mischievous.

Home was a place where I basically ate, slept, and spent time with my siblings. We enjoyed each other's company. There were six of us at home now. Another older sister had married and started her own family. My sister and I were close, so I visited her often. I loved my brother-in-law. He was also fond of me. He was a good man. He passed away at an early age, and his death had a profound effect on me. Death and its effect bothered me tremendously as a kid.

We didn't attend church, hardly ever. I didn't know anything about God, so when things went wrong, I handled it the best way I knew how. As a child and teenager, I had so many questions about life. Mom was at home more now than before. It wasn't like she could sit down with me and answer my questions, and I had a lot of them.

In those days, growing up, we could have used all the branches of psychiatry. Because of the negative influences that I had as a child, my personality and character, or lack thereof, were already developed.

The only real challenge that I had at home was dealing with Mom's men friends. Things would be going just fine until these married men came calling. At times, it comes back to my remembrance even to this day. Our minds are computers, not erasers. What goes in is photocopied and stored for future use.

The year was winding down. I was adjusting to junior high, always excited about life. I started to grow up somewhat and began to pursue relationships with the opposite sex—yes, girls. Junior high is not the place to start dating, but I did! Most men/boys equate liking a girl or dating with sex, and at that young age, it often ends up being uncontrolled intercourse.

By the end of the school year, I had dated several girls in what we used to call puppy love. Nothing too serious.

I want to say this to parents: psychological abuse and child neglect can still take place even though there are two parents in the home. All children need assurance, affirmation, guidance, and security. They need to be told that they are special, they need to be told that they are loved, and they need to be held at times in the arms of both mother and father. Children are not cookie cutters, meaning that they are not all alike; they are different. They see things from different lenses, they don't all think alike, and they all too often duplicate or copy what their parents do.

Being a parent is no joke. All too often, parents seem to think that as long as my child or children have a roof over their head, food to eat, nice clothes, live in affluent neighborhoods, and all of those outside stuff, they should be happy. Let me tell you something, parents. Your child needs you. You can have three doctorates, six masters, and nine degrees of bachelor of science—you need to bring everything that the Almighty has equipped you with to the table when raising children.

I read something years ago that goes,

> Amateur rules on how to learn to be a parent. Number one: Accept the fact that being a parent is one of the most important tasks you will ever undertake and budget your time and energy accordingly. Number two: Think long and hard about the particular role you have to play "now", you can't go back and do it over again! Number three: Don't regard your child as an extension of yourself. Number four: Enjoy your children. Number five: Love and believe in them. Number six: Expect something of your children. Number seven: Be honest with them. Number eight: Let them go. We don't own our children. In the end, the best we can do for them is to free them into the hands of God. (This was written by a former college president)

Seventh grade had been a challenge in many ways, but I made it through, a little battered and bruised. I was a teenager. More often than not, we seem to bounce back.

The end of the seventh grade came to a close. I have been promoted to the eighth grade. Now it gets a little fuzzy. My eighth-grade teacher was either Ms. Pearson or Mr. Whiteside. I could have asked some of my former classmates, but at the time of writing my story, after fifty-plus years, some of them had passed away, moved out of state, or just didn't want to be bothered. My junior-high years were between the years of 1972 and 1975.

Let me just say this: to be free from your past, you must find someone, something bigger than humanity, a cause that supersedes anything that Planet Earth can offer, someone whom life itself cannot fathom. Not a train, not a bullet, not a fast-speeding locomotive—he's got to be a superman.

Eighth grade started out a little brighter than expected. I had matured *some* from the following year and seemingly making better choices. My best friend Tom and I spent a lot of time together at home and in school. We were inseparable. I was six months older than him and enjoyed his friendship. We were like two peas in a pod. That year, Tom and I made the varsity football team, though Tom was in ninth grade, and I was in eighth grade. The grade difference didn't bother me then. I just felt like I belonged. I was finally hanging out and playing with my age group.

At this time in my life, I really enjoyed going to school. I had made other friends from the Parkwood and surrounding neighborhoods as well. A lot of us played on the varsity football team and were pretty close. I loved coming to school. Tom and I were so silly. Sometimes we would dress up in raggedy clothes and go to school like that. Getting on the school bus would get us some laughs. At other times, we would go to school dressed to a tee—sharp as a pencil, as they say.

My teenage years were filled with fun and excitement. I really didn't concern myself with other people's challenges or problems. I was just enjoying life, basically doing what I thought made me happy.

Eastway was a good school from the principal. Not so much the assistant principal, Mr. Mitchell, whom I didn't care too much for, but I respected him for his toughness.

In the '60s and '70s, when you got into trouble at school, the teachers used to do the disciplining—yes, whipping your butt. In junior high school, the discipline was often administered by the assistant principal—yes, Mr. Mitchell! He would usually give you three licks. Man, he could give or administer very well. I really think that he enjoyed his job.

In my opinion, when they removed prayer and corporal punishment out of our school system, the character of our children declined. Our parents gave their approval. When you were sent to the office for disciplinary action, you had two choices: either take the three licks or get-out-of-school suspension. If you got suspended, your Mom had to bring you back to school, and living with Thelma Ivey—I mean, who had to miss work to bring you back to school—you often just took the whipping.

When you enter middle adolescence, fourteen to sixteen years old, you think that you are grown and know everything. These are really the years when you need parental guidance. Eastway was full of positive influences. Mr. Braswell and Mrs. Bynum were school counselors; Ms. Robinson, guidance teacher; Mr. Wyatt, physical education and health; Ms. Johnson, occupational instruction; and Mr. Jenkins, eighth- and ninth-grade math, just to name a few. They genuinely cared about the students, black or white, and we knew it.

Talk about genuineness, there was a television series called *The Waltons*, which aired on September 14, 1972. It featured a Virginia family during the Depression. I loved watching that television series anytime that I got a chance. It was a good, influential television show. It featured black families as well.

The dad Walton was always willing to give a hand whenever possible. I relished seeing Grandpa and Grandma. They could hold their own. One of my favorite moments in watching the show was when the family would sit down for breakfast or supper and discuss the day's challenges. Pop Walton and Ma Walton were always willing and ready to listen to the children's concerns, from the youngest to the eldest. That included, yes, John Boy.

How I longed to come home and sit around the table with Mom and my siblings after a challenging day at school or just being able to express what was going on inside of me. The eighth grade was probably the best time of my life, relative to my teenage years in school. It was a time in my life that I was experiencing being alive. I was coming into my own, so to speak. This would be the last year that I would enjoy hanging around my age group, which was very important for me. I loved socializing with my peers at school, at home, or in the neighborhood.

I can remember the house parties that we would have on the weekends. There was a party over there, a party over here, and a party everywhere. I even had a couple parties at my house after the begging and pleading with Mom.

Well, having attended one of those parties is how I met or became friendly with my first real girlfriend. I was already dating a young lady before this time, but she wasn't at this particular party. Back then, we loved to dance to fast music but enjoyed the slow music even better. At these home parties, we would spike the punch, meaning alcohol was added. Yes, at fourteen, fifteen, and sixteen years old, we were drinking.

The night that I began dating my first real girlfriend, I had gotten a little tipsy or drunk. I had a little too much to drink and started slow dragging, as we called it back then, where one thing led to another. After the music was over, one of the boys came over to me and said that the young lady wanted me to walk her home. I could barely walk myself. That was the beginning of a long courtship that would last for many years.

Over the years of growing up, I had become more and more disrespectful of Mom, having been exposed to the different men in her life. Mothers, take note. It really has a lasting effect on your sons when they see you with different men. They learn to disrespect women as they grow up.

As eighth grade began to wind down, I began to think about ninth grade, as my peers would be moving on to senior high at Garinger High School. Being at Eastway Junior High was fun while it lasted. I was going to be turning sixteen years old come June 1, 1974. Although I would be in ninth grade, I could take driver's education at Garinger High School in the summer, so I signed up for the summer class. Little did I know, a lot of the neighborhood teenagers had signed up for driver's education.

Well, the school year came to an end. There I was back where I started, seemingly with my little sister and friends. Having stayed back in first grade would haunt me tremendously. It might not affect some children, but it did me.

The summer of 1974 was full of fun, hanging out with friends, attending parties, just enjoying life. Driver's education classes had started, so I did settle down long enough to attend classes at Garinger. I was eager to get my driver's license, so I studied my books intensely. After the classroom, came the freedom driver training course. We were allowed to drive by ourselves. The course was set up to resemble a street with stop signs, stoplights—the whole nine yards. For a teenager, this was heaven.

The Freedom Driving Range is where the Mecklenburg school system sent students from all over the city to practice our driving skills. My girlfriend at the time was also in my driver's education class, so you know that I had to impress her. I was such a show-off.

Well, the driver's education class was coming to a close, and it was test time. As I can remember, I scored the second highest in the class. I was really proud of the milestone. I got my driver's certificate, and the next day, I went and got my learner's permit and took the test. I took the test for my driver's license the following day and flunked by a point or so. Yes, you guessed it. I went back after a day or so and passed the test. Wow, I was a happy sailor.

After getting my driver's license in the summer of 1974, I literally lost my mind. I started doing things that I wouldn't have dreamed of before. At sixteen years old and driving my sister's and brother's cars, I attracted attention from my neighborhood friends. We loved driving through the neighborhood and just hanging out. I was sexually active, so you can imagine what I was using the vehicles for.

The summer of '74 was coming to an end. School was about to start, and my peers were heading to Garinger High School. And I? I was going back to Eastway Junior High. Sixteen years old with a driver's license. Wow!

CHAPTER 8

CRIME DOES NOT PAY: SIX MONTHS IN JAIL

That summer, before school started, I had become close friends with another teenager who was a year younger than me. Although my best friend Tom and I would sort of drift in other directions, I still considered him my best friend. This new friend and I started getting into trouble. He and I had some of the same devilish desires—making money by getting into criminal activity. We had previously hung out with some older guys who were holding up or robbing people who sold pot or marijuana.

This didn't last, but for a brief period, we started stealing tires from car dealerships, breaking and entering, and eventually, armed robbery, so when school started in the fall of 1974 and Tom had started at Garinger High School, this new friend and I became close friends. Actually, we became partners in crime. Both of us were supposed to be going back for our ninth-grade year at Eastwood Junior High, but because I was driving now, we probably spent more time visiting Garinger than being at Eastway. That was where most of our friends were our age.

One of the biggest, if not the biggest, mistakes that school year that I made was my girlfriend at sixteen years old had become pregnant. Wow! That was September 1974. I didn't realize that she was pregnant. She had also moved on to Garinger and was now in tenth grade. She was in band at the time and would be sick most of the time. This was devastating for me. Sixteen years old, no job, and still in junior high, man. I would try to work on jobs that hired at sixteen years old, but I was so unstable they wouldn't last long. For the first time in my middle teenage life, I began to experience fear, uncertainty, and a loss of purpose. I didn't spend a lot of time at home during this time, so Mom didn't fully know what I was doing. My eldest siblings had moved out of the house, and I was now the eldest at home. Looking back now, I was not a good example for my three younger siblings.

I was still immature and messing around with other girls. I didn't realize the seriousness of becoming a teenage father. My world was crumbling around me. It seemed that there was nowhere or no one that I could turn to. My partner in crime and I became bolder and bolder at robbery.

I didn't attend school much at Eastway. In fact I didn't even remember my assigned homeroom teacher. In previous years, I looked forward to being in the yearbook. This year was different. From the summer of 1974 through the spring of 1975, I was constantly doing whatever I pleased. I was out of control. I don't remember being home much because home, for me, wasn't a safe place to be—Mom and her men!

I believe with all my heart that the biggest turning point in my teenage years was the time living on Parkwood Avenue. It's when I walked in on Mom having sex with one of her men. I turned on the light, and to my surprise, it wasn't one of the filthy married men. It was a third man. The worst part about the encounter was that although looking into their faces, Mom said the woman I saw wasn't her. How stupid could I be? You talk about anger. I lost it. That was the first time that I ever cursed Mom.

Can you imagine sixteen years old? Girlfriend pregnant, no plans, and full of anger. My partner in crime and I had broken into this one house where he had found a twelve-gauge shotgun. Unbeknownst to him, there was a live shotgun shell in the chamber. We were playing around when he pointed the gun at my head and pulled the latch back and said, "Horace, I'm going to shoot you. Just playing."

I said to him, "Boy, stop playing around."

At that very moment, the shotgun turned downward to the floor. He pulled the trigger and blew a six- to eight-inch hole in the floor.

That wasn't the last time that I had a near-death experience. I had become comfortable with guns, so I kept some around me most of the time. I remember one time in the fall of 1975, my sister and I didn't go to school that day. I was counting some money on the floor. Earlier, she had observed me cleaning a pistol. At that time, there were no bullets in the pistol or the gun.

Well, I put the bullets back in the pistol, but she didn't know it. As she came back into the room, she noticed that the gun was lying on the dresser. She picked up the gun and pointed it toward my back, and just playing around, she said, "Brother, I'm going to shoot you." At that very moment, the gun turns toward the floor, and she pulled the trigger. The bullet lodged into the carpet. Sound familiar?

All through my ninth-grade school year, there were these kinds of life-and-death situations happening to me. My partner in crime and I would continue breaking and entering for a while but eventually stopped that and started the robberies instead. Again, not attending school, hanging out, going to parties on the weekends, the girls, etc.

My girlfriend, being pregnant in high school, finally had to attend a school for young teenage mothers called TAPS. To my surprise, there were other girls in the neighborhood who had gotten pregnant also and attending TAPS. Because of my uncontrolled lifestyle, I mistreated her, something awfully bad. The years 1974 through 1975 will be the worst of my teenage life up until then.

My partner in crime and I would continue our crime spree all throughout our ninth-grade school year. Coming up into the spring of 1975, another one of my teenage friends and I tried to attend night school with no success. One of my teachers at the time informed me that Eastwood Junior High was endeavoring to have me excluded from the school for the rest of the year.

After committing several robberies during that fall, winter, and spring, my partner and I committed a robbery in our neighborhood at a community store where the store clerk was shot. After not being caught for the other crimes that we had committed after almost a year, our days of living life like gangsters were finally coming to an end! All the bad seeds that I had sown were about to catch up to me. The disrespect for my mom, my girlfriend, and humanity itself was closing in on me. This was in the springtime of May 1975. There was now a warrant out for my arrest. I knew that the police would eventually catch up to me, so I didn't spend much time at home.

One day, as I was walking through the neighborhood, a police officer stopped me and asked me my name. I gave him a friend's name and address who lived on the same street as I did, so after questioning me for a few minutes, he let me go. I continued to avoid being caught for about two more weeks. I continued to evade the police.

One Saturday night as I was at a party, my sister who was three years older than me somehow got into contact with me and told me that my girlfriend at that time had gone into the hospital, and my child was born. It was a girl born on May 17, 1975. Well, I continued to party, not knowing the gravity of what had happened. I was now a sixteen-year-old father! I didn't immediately go see my newborn child, but when I did, I remember taking a baby seat and a few other items.

All through my courtship with my daughter's mother, I neglected her and caused her much pain and embarrassment and shame even to this day as I write this book. Please forgive me. I was wrong.

Well, after about two weeks of dodging the police, one beautiful late-spring day, May 28, 1975, a couple of friends and I were walking up North Allen Street, passing Saint Paul's Baptist Church, when several police cars surrounded me, demanding I stop. They put handcuffs on me. It was the same officer whom I had given the false information to two weeks earlier, and he reminded me of the incident. My days of crime had ended. As I look back, it was really a relief. All that time of living out of control had finally come to an end. Mom had prophesied, "Son, one day, you will wish that you could be home, and you will not be able to." Mom's prophecy had finally come to pass.

As I was being arrested, my sister was somehow passing by as the police were putting me into the back seat of the vehicle, yelling, "What are you all doing to my brother? He hasn't done anything." Little did my sister or my family know that I was long due for this day. Until that day, May 28,1975, I had never spent a day in jail.

It was like a nightmare. I couldn't believe that this was happening to me. It was on a Wednesday afternoon when I was arrested. The police officers drove me uptown to Fourth Street, where I was taken into the jail or police department, fingerprinted, and put into a holding cell. I was wearing a red-and-white jersey with the number 44 on it, a pair of maroon terry cloth–like pants, long white socks, and a pair of white Chuck Taylor tennis shoes, as I can recall. I had my supernatural Afro. Yes, I can remember it like it was yesterday. As I sat there in that holding cell, looking around, I just couldn't believe that it was real. I thought, *I'll just go to sleep, and when I wake up, the dream would be over, and I would be at home.* Remember Dorothy and Toto in *The Wizard of Oz*?

Well, after several hours of being in the holding cell, I awakened from my sleep and realized that this was not a dream. Realizing that this was a turning point in my life, all of the foolishness and the hurt that I had caused others began to surface. Fear, uncertainty, and just not knowing what was happening to me gripped my entire being.

Up until then, I didn't know anything about God. I would hear Mom sing some of the old Negro hymns. I would visit Parkwood CME Church with my best friend Tom occasionally. I enjoyed going to church when I did go, but I never became a member. Tom's family was actively involved in the church during this time. Well, finally, about two or three o'clock on Thursday morning, May 29, three days before my seventeenth birthday, which would be June 1, 1975, a sheriff deputy came to the holding cell and escorted me into the area where I would be given my jailhouse attire, bed linen, shoes, and other toiletries.

I had to surrender my street clothes and dress out into the jailhouse attire, which, at the time, I believe was orange. I was carried to a cell on the upper floor, where teenagers were held. With my bed linen and rubber mattress in hand, I was led to this new cell, where a couple of officers were manning the floor. The door to the cell was open, and I walked in on these other teenage boys who were already asleep, being that it was only about two or three o'clock in the morning. The cell was dark and quiet. Young boys were sleeping on the floor. The inner cell beds were already full, so I had to put my rubber bedding on top of the steel table located in the middle of the cell. The steel table was also used to eat on and set around to rest. Still living this nightmare, I managed to go to sleep somehow.

After sleeping what seemed to me an eternity, I was awakened by all the noises of young boys preparing for breakfast. I woke up with these other teenagers everywhere. They were lined up, as it were, receiving metal trays of food through these trapdoors, where food and other items would be handed to us. It was between the hours of five or maybe six o'clock in the morning when breakfast was served. As I looked around and observed my surroundings, I couldn't believe that this was actually happening.

I was literally sick on my stomach, as they say. I've always been a big kid, so I didn't have to concern myself about being taken advantage of. After setting up on the mattress or cart, one of the boys who was handing the breakfast trays around asked me if I wanted my tray. I told him that he could have it. I was in no condition to eat anything. I was in a daze. I couldn't think. All reasoning was gone. Had I died and gone to the hot place? What was happening to me on the inside of my being couldn't come close to what I had ever experienced the first sixteen years of my life. This was traumatic at its worst. That whole day was like hell had swallowed me up. I didn't pay attention to the faces around me. The pain that gripped my insides was unbearable. I was physically able to make it to those steel doors, knocking as hard as I could, asking for help.

I thought I was losing my mind at sixteen years old. What did I know about going crazy? I was crying, begging for help, "Please, please, someone help me." I don't know to this day what the other teens were saying or thinking, but none of them ever approached me. I don't remember how long this went on, but I was truly like a wild black stallion being broken, like a woman having a baby, which I've seen several times. My God, what is happening to me? Whatever I had sown, I was reaping it right then sevenfold.

Many days would pass, and I don't remember turning seventeen years old. That wasn't even my concern. I just wanted the pain to go away. The sheriff deputies never bothered me during those episodes. I guess it was God's way of saying, "I am God, and there is none greater!"

Let me say this: I don't care who you think you are or where you come from. If you don't humble yourself, God Almighty has a way to humble you. I stand as a living witness.

Well, days and weeks went by. I began to settle down, realizing the depth of what had happened. The robbery with a deadly weapon, which I was charged two counts with, was beginning to become a reality. The white man didn't do this to me. I did the crimes, and now it was my time to pay the debt.

When you are arrested, you will be given the charges that you are charged with. I don't know how they do it nowadays, but back then in 1975, they would bring your paperwork to your cell. Weeks passed by. I finally got my first visitors. Who? You guessed it—my Mom and my girlfriend. I had somehow gotten to a place where I was ready to handle visitors and was very happy and relieved to see Mom.

Up until this time, I didn't know what was going on in regard to the legal aspects of the charges brought against me. Mom told me that she and my eldest sister were working on getting me a lawyer. I didn't need a lawyer. I wanted to get out of jail. That was my thinking.

The visit went well. Mom was visibly hurt but managed to smile as she would say, "You are still my child, and I'm here for you."

And as for my girlfriend, I was so ashamed of the way that I had treated her during her pregnancy. Seeing other girls, the disrespect for her, now she was on the other side of the thick glass window, saying that she loved me. I was crushed.

The visit being over, I was taken back to my cell. I had pretty much gotten adjusted to being locked up by now. Again, I was seventeen years old then. Teenagers should be able to bounce back quicker than adults. We haven't experienced most of the challenges that they have faced yet.

I had become familiar with most of the other boys in my cell, although new boys would be coming and going at this point. There wasn't much for us to do but talk. You get to know each other's charges. I was even getting to know some of the boys from other parts of Charlotte. Some of them I went to school with. Having been charged with such serious crimes, my bail was set high. I believe at the time, around $20,000. It may just as well have been $1 million. I wasn't getting out of jail.

I started reading books that boys had left behind when they were released from jail. Before I was arrested, I was lifting weights when I wasn't playing football or boxing. As a matter of fact, I would box for several months, eventually participating in the 1972 Golden Gloves. A lot of teenagers would join the neighborhood boxing team. I even got my best friend Tom to join. I was always participating in some sport.

Now being locked up, I started working out almost daily, doing hundreds of push-ups and sit-ups. You name it, and I was doing it. The other boys respected me, and I looked to them at times for comfort and support. Boys will be boys, so there would be fights most of the time. I would kind of monitor the fights, making sure that they were fair. Don't get me wrong. We were teenage criminals. Some of us had been involved in serious crimes, including murder. There were black and white inmates in my cell from all walks of life, and some of us were dangerous.

I finally got a visit from my lawyer. My Mom and sister had hired a pretty good law firm—Plumides, Plumides, and Schuster—which at the time was well known. I believe that the gentleman who visited me was Mike Plumides. Nonetheless, he assured me that they would represent me to the fullest extent. I was so embarrassed about what I had done, the shame. In fact, it was quite some time before I could honestly own up to the shooting. I wasn't known for lying, but for the first time in my teenage life, I wasn't telling the whole truth, so help me God.

It was now summertime. School was out, and my friends on the outside were living it up! I would get news from home while talking on the phone. We were allowed to make phone calls periodically. I would try and keep up with my now-estranged girlfriend from jail. Right! With what she had gone through with me, and now with an infant child to care for, please.

She hadn't yet turned seventeen and now just going to the eleventh grade. Looking back, I can only imagine what she was going through. It's so amazing how, when a young boy or man gets in trouble with the law and is locked away, we try to control women on the outside.

While months passed by, I had been to court several times, pleading not guilty, with my lawyer by my side and some family members in the courtroom. I would hope to get a chance to just glance at them. Let me say this: for me, jail was worse than prison.

I finally settled down. This is where I was going to be for a while. I started reading whatever I could get my hands on. I wanted to stay occupied with whatever I could. I wasn't a spiritually minded person at the time. Mom would encourage me to pray, and she gave me scriptures to read. One of my favorite scriptures to this day is Psalm 27. Mom would say, "Now you read these scriptures every day."

There would be white men from churches who'd come visit with the inmates at times. This is where I would be introduced to the little tracks called *Our Daily Bread*. There would be updated ones occasionally, so I would finish one and start another.

At this time in my life, I knew that I needed a change. Weeks and months would continue to come and go. It seemed like an eternity. One particular day, as I was reading a copy of *Our Daily Bread*, at the back of the book was—at the time, I didn't know—what was called the sinner's prayer. It said that if I would confess my sins, that he, Jesus, would forgive me for my sins, and he would become my Savior and Lord. I repeated out of my mouth that prayer. I didn't know anything about God, Jesus, or anyone else, but I tell you the truth, that very minute, something happened on the inside of my being that I know, God had answered my prayer.

I got a hold of a Bible somehow and began reading it every day. I didn't know much about God, but I began telling the other boys about Jesus and started having Bible study.

That experience turned my life in the right direction. I didn't change overnight, but my heart became much more empathetic, showing an ability to understand and share the feelings of others. I was no longer self-centered.

As the months passed by, I had gone to court on several different occasions. My lawyers were keeping me informed on what was happening in the courtroom. In the jail cell, I began working on myself more, studying, praying (yes, praying), reading, and exercising.

Six months of being in jail was now approaching. It was now October 1975. School had started, so I didn't hear too much from the outside world. Meanwhile, it was finally my day in court. This was the big one, as Fred Sanford used to say.

I went into the courtroom that October day, not knowing what was going to happen, but I was glad that something would happen. As I entered the courtroom, I sat beside my lawyer, shook his hand, looked around the courtroom, and saw some familiar faces. The district attorney and my attorney had evidently made a plea agreement that I would be charged as a youthful offender, not a regular offender. This meant that I would be sent to a youth correctional facility instead of an adult prison.

Nonetheless, the proceedings continued after the motions were heard. The judge had my lawyer and me stand up, along with the district attorney and his team. The judge pronounced the sentence. I was given twelve to fifteen years in prison but could serve one day to fifteen years. As I heard the verdict, my heart sank, tears rolled down my cheeks, and it was finally over. No more waiting or guessing, and I could now begin to start paying back at least some of the bad seed that I had sown.

As I turned toward my lawyer. I saw Mom coming up beside him. She was allowed to come hug me with that smile that she always had even when she was hurting. She said to me, "You be a good boy."

Court had now ended, and I was taken back to the cell where I had spent most of the almost six months. As I entered the cell, the other boys were coming up to me, asking, "What happened in the courtroom?" This was what we did after anyone of us would return from court. I told them I had been sentenced to twelve to fifteen years as a committed youthful offender, not an adult. But for God's mercy, I could have gotten a longer sentence. Even in our mess, God still shows us his mercy.

I had been sentenced early in the week, so I didn't know exactly when I would be shipped out or even where I was being shipped to. Having received my sentence, I could now begin concentrating on doing whatever it took to get my life in order and start the rehabilitation process. With God being in my life, I had a clear path to follow. I was now seventeen years old and had matured greatly in six months.

That week, I began saying goodbyes to the boys. We were sort of family, having spent much of our time together.

Well, Friday, the morning of October 17, 1975, I was asked to get my stuff packed. I was being shipped out. I did as I was instructed. The clothes that I had worn on the twenty-eighth day of May, when I was arrested, were the clothes that I was given to be shipped out wearing. The deputy sheriff led me to two white men awaiting me to take me to Piedmont Western Correctional Center located in Morganton, North Carolina. From the time that we got into the county vehicle, these men showed me kindness and respect. The drive to Morganton was a pleasant trip. Even then, God had begun to work in my life.

If you notice from the beginning of my writing, I didn't mention much, if anything, about God, so from this point on I am going to endeavor not to make the book a religious narrative, but I have to give glory to the one who allowed me to be here—God. I ask for your indulgence.

It was a beautiful day on the Friday of October 17, 1975. I had been locked up in jail for close to six months. For a seventeen-year-old teenager, that was seemingly a lifetime. As we drove on the highway heading toward the mountains, the two men who had picked me up from the Mecklenburg County Jail was having different conversations about their jobs, family hunting, and about life. It fascinated me. I was eager to hear anything new after listening to all the jailhouse talk.

The scenery was beautiful, and the sun was shining brightly. It was mid-October, so it hadn't turned cold. The weather was superb. For such a long time from my youth up until now, I hadn't experienced such a peace inside. Not knowing where we were going, the drive seemed like hours. It didn't really matter. I was free in a sense. The drive was actually about one hour and thirty minutes.

CHAPTER 9

LIFE AT THE HIGH RISE: EIGHT MONTHS IN PRISON

As we got closer to the Western Correctional Center, the roads became winding as we made our way toward the sixteen-story high-rise building. I could see the building from a distance. It reached up into the sky. It looked like a hotel in the middle of nowhere.

We finally began to enter the center. It was located in what looked like the bottom of a mountain on the left side. We drove up to the center, where there were cows—yes, cows, a lot of them. The view was serene, and we pulled up into the parking lot. The two men opened my door and let me out. It felt good being outside, and we walked toward the entrance of the building. I looked up at the high-rise building that resembled a hotel, and I was simply amazed. This would be my home for the next eight months.

Once we entered the building, there was a lobby where the center's employees would walk back and forth to offices situated on the first floor. It didn't look like a prison. It was far from being like the jail where I had spent almost six months. For me, it was a new beginning.

As we walked through the lobby, there was an electric gate—bars, as it were—that opened for the three of us. The two men surrendered their weapons as we came to this point. They were making conversation with other officers as we passed by different stages of the building. I was escorted to the back of the building, where I began the process of changing out of my street clothes. As I entered the change-out area, we were taken through a cleaning area, where we were showered down with a cleaning solution. After drying off, we were handed our prison clothes. At the time, I didn't know the difference between felony and honor grade. I was a convicted felon and was given gray clothing. I liked the green ones too but would not get those until later.

After telling the officers in charge our sizes, we, meaning the other boys who had arrived that same day but on buses from all over the state, were escorted to an area where we dressed and put on our state-issued socks and shoes. It was more like going into the military as opposed to being in prison.

The high-rise had sixteen floors. As we entered the facility, we were assigned to the thirteenth floor. That was where we would be given our classification upon being placed on any floor within the high-rise. You were given a folder to take with you wherever you went throughout the facility. We had to maintain a certain number of points each month to either stay on that floor or move to a lower floor, which meant greater privileges.

Going up higher wasn't good. That meant that you weren't following orders or disrespecting the officers. It could be easy for anyone who was interested in getting their life on track, and that happened to be me. I made up my mind that jail and prison weren't the life for me, and from day one, I followed the rules and regulations.

I tell you the truth, I lie not. Western Correctional Institution was one of the best things that could have happened to me. While there, the foundation, structure, and discipline that I needed to be a productive human being was taking place on the inside of my being. It was there at the high-rise that I started developing godly character.

The very first day that I arrived at this facility, I began taking advantage of every opportunity afforded me. One was respecting authority; another was following instructions, something that I didn't do well at home with Mom. I will say this and make no apology: when our young black boys can't respect our parents, whether they are two-parent homes or single-parent homes, government and our society will surely have a place for them. Hopefully, our young boys and young men won't lose their lives in the process.

I was put on the elevator and taken to the thirteenth floor. As I got to the floor, I stepped out into what was called the dayroom. This was a large open room where the boys or young men would sit when they weren't in their rooms. Each floor that we lived on had four hallways. Each hallway had, if I can remember, twelve rooms, a wash area, and a shower area. One thing that really impressed me was how clean the facility was. Not only did most of the young men keep themselves clean and groomed, but the building stayed clean also.

Upon stepping off the elevator, I was assigned a room on C hall. It was around lunchtime, so I carried my bed linen and toiletries to my room. Each room usually had a bed and a cabinetlike table, which had a light on it. Also, there would be a chair, where you could sit on while you were in your room.

I hurried back into the big dayroom, where the rest of the inmates were. Meals were served in this open space. There were tables and chairs that accommodated at least forty-eight young men. Our meals would be delivered to us on food carts. Every floor was served this way. As the food cart arrived, the officers would help take the carts off of the elevators. There was an officer's station situated on each floor of the high-rise. The officers' station was enclosed with glass so that they could see what was happening in the dayroom. As the food cart entered the room, the officer would assign a young man to help serve our meal. There were usually two officers on each floor.

After breakfast, lunch, and dinner were over, we would usually be sent to our rooms. The officer would pick out certain boys to help clean up after each meal. The whole floor would be cleaned, mopped, and wiped down. This was called extra duty, and you could earn points to make your months total to stay on that floor.

Remember, it's been almost fifty years ago since I've been out of the high-rise, so if I don't get everything to a tee, believe me, it's very close. I arrived in Morganton the weekend of October 17, and that Friday was a long day as I observed my surroundings. I got to know a lot of the other boys that day. Some of them had been locked up with me in the Mecklenburg County Jail. It was always good to be surrounded by your homeboys, as we addressed each other. I quickly developed some good habits as the days passed by, like not sitting around the dayroom too long. Most of the boys would sit out watching TV or playing cards, checkers, chess, etc. Remember, this was the intake floor, where you got your orientation, the dos and don'ts. Again, I say being at the Western Correctional Youth Institute was really a blessing.

In the weeks ahead, I settled in, and things began to look bright for me. All of the inmates, as we were addressed sometimes, would be assigned a counselor. Any questions, concerns, or problems that we had, we could ask permission to see them. This was a far cry from being in jail for six months. I mean, really. Thank God for my Mom and my big sister. They had sacrificed their financial resources to hire attorneys who helped me get to this place. I never got a chance to experience hard-core prison. I was a teenager who had made bad choices, not a career criminal. Sometimes youngsters do things in their early lives that can haunt them for the rest of their lives, but teenagers who have proper role models, no matter who or where they are, can make a turnaround if they choose to do so.

One attribute that I possess was resilience, being able to bounce back from what seemingly would destroy someone else. I would owe that to my ninety-seven-year-old mother. Mom never quit or gave up on any of her children. No matter the challenge, Mom would find a way.

I don't remember how long I stayed on the thirteenth floor, maybe a month or two. At any rate, I began working the system. I was determined to do what I had to do in regard to making my stay at the high-rise productive.

Everywhere I went, I carried my folder with me. Again, that was how we would be accounted for while we were off our home floor. It was very important how we dressed and presented ourselves. Whether visiting our counselors, going to the gym, or visiting the chaplain, we weren't just sitting around. We were actually building the character and maturing into young adults.

I don't remember when I moved down to the lower floor, but having made my points and higher than needed, I was moved to the tenth floor. Back then, if my memory serves me right, gray clothes could only go to the ninth floor. Each month, I was making higher points. It was a challenge for most of us. We all would be ready for extra duty when given the opportunity. Once on the tenth floor, I knew that I could get a job within the facility, so I visited my counselor, and he got me classified into the kitchen. I had to talk to one of the staff who ran the kitchen at the time. I entered his office that day. He quizzed me on kitchen etiquette and talked about different recipes. Afterward, I was given a measurement test relating to how much it would take to feed around 450 teenagers plus staff.

Well, I passed the test. Thanks to Mom for allowing me to be in the kitchen watching her cook. I became the head cook for the second shift. It was a big responsibility, but I rose to the challenge. I loved cooking. We used huge everything—pots, frying pans, and deep fryers. Remember, I was cooking for more than 450-plus people.

I was visiting my counselor one day and happened to pass by a classroom where the instructor, a teacher from Western Piedmont Community College, would conduct GED classes. I peeked into the room and noticed a copy of a GED diploma. Yes, you got that right. I immediately signed up for the class. Wow! I stayed occupied. I would hardly be on the tenth floor. I would be working in school or working out in the weight room. I only used my room to sleep in. Each night I returned from the kitchen, I would take the time to read my Bible, besides preparing for the GED exam.

I enjoyed being back in school. This time I could focus on continuing my education without any outside influences. It was a good time in my life. I could finally be a teenager without all the drama and clutter that I dealt with back in Charlotte. My mind was now clear to concentrate on myself. I wasn't concerned and didn't have to be about Mom, my siblings, or as selfish as it sounds, the estranged girlfriend and my infant child. This was my time, my opportunity to get things right so that I could help my loved ones I left behind.

Western Correctional Institute was, what I believe to this day, God's way of saying, "Boy, I have given you a second chance to a new and brighter future. Don't blow it."

Well, I didn't. My days were regimented. For the eight months that I was at the high-rise, each day was accounted for. It was like being in the military. I never had a problem with any of the officers. It was so satisfying having the structure and discipline that being locked up afforded me.

Once I started working in the kitchen, it would be around two or three o'clock in the afternoon, if memory serves me right, because dinner was served around five o'clock. There were other young men on my shift also. We had a baker as well. All of us worked well together. Every night before leaving the kitchen to go to our floors or rooms, the kitchen had to be cleaned. The floor was steam cleaned every night. When we left the kitchen, it would be spotless.

I worked in the kitchen seven days a week. I remember once, it was a day that I was frying chicken, I would usually put some seasoning on my chicken and into the flour that made the chicken have a great taste. I would also put butter in with my oil. Man, you could smell the aroma all throughout the kitchen, even outside on the second floor, which was where the kitchen was located. That particular day, the headman in charge of the whole facility, Major Jarvis, came into the kitchen. He came over to me and started a conversation with me. He asked me my name, and I told him, "Horace Ivey". I fixed him a plate. I think he carried it with him. However, he turned to me and said to write him a letter telling him that he had a talk with me that day in the kitchen.

Well, not long after that meeting with the superintendent Major Javas, I made honor grade. That meant I no longer wore the gray felony uniforms. I was given the green uniform, representing honor and fulfilling the required duties and obligations that was expected of me. The honor grade enabled me to be given a level 3 security clearance, which meant more freedom within and outside the high-rise. With that honor, I could move down to the lowest floor possible within the prison there at the high-rise.

While working in the kitchen, I enrolled into the GED class. There were three levels that you could enter. Level 1 was beginners, level 2 was intermediate, and level 3 advanced, at this level is when you were ready or prepared to take the actual GED exam. I don't remember what month I enrolled in the class, but I do remember painstakingly studying the required courses. I had always wanted to finish school, and this was my chance. As I stated earlier in the book, I had stayed back a grade in elementary school, first grade, so I was behind my peers. This bothered me all through my childhood. Being in first grade with my little sister wasn't something that I was comfortable with. Now I had the opportunity to get my high school diploma two years ahead of my little sister. It wasn't something that I considered at the time, but hey.

The months passed by quickly. I stayed the course, doing what was required and expected of me. Life was grand. During my stay at the high-rise, I would work out in the gymnasium, which was located on the first floor. When I wasn't working in the kitchen or attending GED classes, I spent time lifting weights. I had always worked out with weights, even at home. My best friend Tom and I would lift weights in his backyard, we loved it. When Tom and I wasn't working out together; I would work out at home in my front hallway. I would send off for workout programs that cost me a dollar or so. That was when the old bodybuilders were going strong Dave Draper, Bill Pearl, Larry Scott, and the man, Arnold Schwarzenegger. I loved bodybuilding and looked forward to competing.

One day while working out in the gymnasium, I met and became good friends with one of the gym coordinators and coaches, Harold Johnson. Harold and I respected each other from the moment we met. Harold, or Mr. Johnson, as we called him, genuinely cared about the young men who came to the high-rise, and we could sense this sincerity in the way that he interacted with us. One day, I was going through a challenge. I forgot what it was. I was usually jovial and playful, but this particular day, I wasn't my usual self. Mr. Johnson recognized the change in my attitude and allowed me to go to my room to chill out. He later came up to my floor to see if all was well. That was the kind of person he was.

After working in the kitchen for several months, which I enjoyed, I wanted a change of pace. We could be reclassified to other positions within the high-rise, so I visited my counselor and did just that. I wanted to work in the gymnasium. Would you have guessed it? The kitchen staff didn't want me to leave, but it was a good move for me. Working in the gym was another good opportunity for me to grow and develop. The staff in the gymnasium—Mr. Blackburn, Mr. Johnson, and one other gentleman—were always so gracious.

I started working out with Mr. Johnson regarding the Presidential Sports Award while there at the Western Correctional Youth Institute. That was an award given by then-president Gerald R. Ford. The program was run by none other than Arnold Schwarzenegger. I excelled in all of the required fitness challenges. Mr. Johnson would keep my time and monitor me through the whole program. I didn't know that he would actually send my results to the administration. Well, months later, Mr. Johnson advised me that I was awarded the Presidential Sports Award, given and signed by none other than President Gerald R. Ford. I still have the award to this day.

Time was moving on, and I would be taking the GED exam soon. It was now entering early spring. I would be turning eighteen years old on June 1, 1976. My time at the high-rise would be coming to an end. Upon turning eighteen, I would have to be shipped to an adult facility.

I took the GED exam around April or May of 1976 and didn't find out the results until June 1976. I passed the exam with flying colors. Oh, what a happy day. I knew that Mom would be proud of me finishing school, so I sent my diploma home to Mom.

The eight months in Morganton, North Carolina, were coming to an end. God had proven himself faithful so many times in my life even when I didn't know him. I had made so many friends there at the high-rise, so many good memories. I had matured.

June 1 finally arrived. I turned eighteen years old. I had been in prison, you may say, for fourteen months. For me, it seemed a lifetime, but who was counting! I started saying my goodbyes because I could be shipped out at any time in June. It's always unsettling when you don't know where you are going. One thing about being locked up, you don't run anything; you belong to the state. You will find that out one way or the other.

I didn't know at the time but was later informed by one of the faculty there at Western Correctional Youth Institution that the same gentleman, Maj. Mack Jarvis, who was instrumental in getting me my honor grade while at the high-rise, was also responsible for getting me sent to the Piedmont region of the state, Gaston County. This was only a stone's throw from Charlotte, the Queen City.

The day that I left the high-rise was a sad one, yet I knew that I was maturing and had to be around late adolescence, groups of men my age, eighteen to twenty-one years old and beyond. The trip to the exchange station, which I don't remember where, I arrived somewhere between Morganton, North Carolina, and Gastonia, North Carolina. There were other buses arriving at that exchange station at the same time that my state bus arrived. Men from other prisons throughout the state prison system would be going and coming from other places.

I remember lying over, so to speak, there for several hours. Hundreds of men would arrive at that station. We stayed there long enough to be served lunch. Then later, certain names were called to get on the bus for the Piedmont area. I didn't know where I was headed, but I got on to the bus headed for the Piedmont.

CHAPTER 10

LIFE IN PRISON NUMBER TWO—GASTON CORRECTION PRISON: ONE YEAR

As we were traveling on the roads and highways, I was trying to get a glimpse of the roadside signs to see any familiar cities or towns. When I couldn't see anything that I was familiar with, I finally decided to sit back and enjoy the ride. We arrived at the Gaston Correctional Center in the late afternoon. As the bus pulled into the prison yard, I could see that there was a one-story brick building with no gates or fence surrounding the facility.

The men were walking outside as if they were at home, so carefree. Some of them were sitting around the brick picnic tables, just shooting the breeze as I got off the bus. Some of the men greeted me as I entered the building. This was a far cry from the high-rise.

It was now June and just beginning to get hot. Some of the men weren't wearing shirts. It was a mixture of black and white inmates. It was a large dome with two sides. There was a large hallway separating the two sides. Bars were on either side with a gate, like doors that could be locked at times, usually at night.

As I walked into the building, I'd be given my bed linen and toiletries and assigned a bed on the left side of the dome. There were no private rooms. This was not Kansas.

There were about at least 125 beds on each side of the dome. I was given a bed on the top bunk alongside my locker. These were men, grown men. I was eighteen now and strong as an ox, so I was respected immediately! But I also showed these older men the same respect. I was tired from traveling and wondering where I was going to be housed for the next year of my stay in Dallas, so I hopped up onto my bed to take a nap.

Late evening was now approaching. Dinner was now being served. We had to walk over to the mess hall to eat our dinner. The mess hall was located in the back of the facility. There was also the canteen, where you could purchase items such as soap, toothpaste, sweets, coffee, sodas, etc.

There was an area where you could lift weights and a basketball court. It was another step to freedom. I could have rested on my laurels that I had achieved at the Western Correctional Youth Institute, but instead, I got busy. Some of the men would come in from the road crew after working from morning till evening. I had a level 3 security clearance, which allowed me to leave the prison, and I joined the road crew.

I was young and full of life. I possessed an abundance of energy. I loved life and wanted to enjoy it no matter where I was. Being locked up afforded me the ability to learn to harness that energy. The discipline and structure that I had received from the high-rise helped guide my stay at Dallas. Getting along with the officers, respecting the other inmates, following the rules and regulations—it was what I had become accustomed to.

Now don't get me wrong. There were times while in prison I had to defend myself physically, and I did so successfully. Because I never started the trouble and was known as a peaceful person, the officers and inmates had my back. As the weeks passed by and because I was close to Charlotte now, I began to get regular visits from family. Mom was so happy that her boy was close to home. Morganton was far away, so I understood why I didn't get regular visits there.

I looked forward to those Sunday visits. It was at Dallas where I finally saw my daughter since being imprisoned, fourteen months. My best friend Tom brought Mom and my daughter to see me. I can't complain about friends visiting me in prison because I didn't have many of them anyway. Tom was my real friend even to this day. I call him friend!

As I got settled in at the Gaston Correctional Center, good things began to happen to me, just as it did in Morganton. The facility was a minimum security prison. Everyone there wore green clothing. They were either honor-grade felons or misdemeanors.

When we advanced to level 4 security status, we were allowed to wear our street clothes. I enjoyed talking with the older men, listening to their prison stories, or just life in general. I had matured greatly and took pride in being at an adult facility. I became close friends with several older men, who were like mentors to me. It was a good time in my development as a young man.

I worked on the road crew for several weeks. There were other men who worked on the road crew also. Each morning, we were given our lunch. We put on our work clothes and shoes and went out to meet the yellow trucks awaiting us. The supervisor of my crew went by the name of Rabbit. That's what the other guys called him. He was a nice old fellow.

It was July now and hot as hades. We would work all up and down the streets and sometimes the highways. We cleared out areas around creek branches. Every day, there was a new location awaiting us. I was young and enjoying every minute of it. It's always good for young men to be occupied and not be idle.

Sometimes when we finished early, Rabbit had a place where he would take us swimming. Evidently, this was a place he'd take others before us. Man, we had fun. At the same time, we were being paid a little something. We were also gaining time off of our sentence.

After working on the road crew that summer of 1976, I was offered a job on the facility working in the canteen. One of the officers, a lieutenant, pulled me to the side one day and asked me if I would be interested in working in the canteen. There was also another young man who would be working with me; his name was Billy. It was a big responsibility involving handling money and inventory.

Like always, I rose to the occasion. I hardly ever thought things through. I just did it. There were always opportunities awaiting me, always favor! Working in the canteen was truly a joy. Billy and I got along well. At times, we had our disagreements but usually worked it out. Sometimes if a man didn't have money, I would just be a blessing and give him whatever he needed. I've always been a giver, always endeavoring to make someone else's life better.

While at the correctional center, I began going to the little church located beside the facility, which would hold services weekly. Different preachers from various churches would come and preach. Other men would attend also. It was just a joy to be able to move about unsupervised most of the time. After working in the canteen for several months, I was promoted to level 4 security clearance. That meant that I had the privilege. You guessed it; I could start having home visits. Yes, after almost eighteen months, I would be going back to Charlotte, North Carolina. I could visit home first six hours, then twelve hours, twenty-four hours, forty-eight hours, and ultimately, seventy-two hours at a time. God had been good to me.

Meanwhile, I could get a job away from the facility, and I did. My first job in over one and a half years. I was finally being allowed to reenter society. I got a job in Gastonia, North Carolina, at Rauch Industries, a Christmas ornament business. There were several of us working there, as I can remember. I was hired for the third shift. I didn't know then, but it was rough. This was the first time that I had ever worked third shift. As a teenager back in Charlotte, I had worked little odd jobs but never third shift. In my reasoning, God never intended for man to stay up after 11:00 p.m., not even animals.

Now that I'm working, it's time for me to pay rent. Yes, I was paying my way now. I even started having money taken out of my check to support my daughter. After all these months, I'm now a responsible parent.

I started working at Rauch Industries around the wintertime. I remember going to work, and it would be cold. I kind of got used to the third shift. Nevertheless, I was able to purchase clothes for my visits home. Each time I got a pass to go home, a different family member would pick me up, and it seemed that they would be late each time, or it might have been I was in a hurry each time to get home.

It became a routine, going to work or going home. A lot of us men at the facility were working and having home passes. Again, I say my stay in prison was like being in the military. Prison was never hard for me. I surrendered.

I began integrating back into normal life, going back to the workforce, getting regular home visits, getting reunited with my family, not so much with old friends. There was a difference in the atmosphere, so to speak. Life doesn't stop because we are out of the picture. The world keeps turning. People change, and they grow up; children are born, people die; and the economy changes. I didn't realize it then, but I had changed.

I was no longer the immature sixteen-year-old boy that I was before going to prison. I had experienced life from a different perspective, a view from another lens. I could think before I leaped or jumped.

As I visited home more and more, I was reunited with my daughter's mother. She had matured also. She had two years without having to put up with me. She had experienced life also from another view, different lenses. I had to get used to my baby girl. She was now two years old. She probably didn't know me from Santa Claus.

Sometimes when I visited home on seventy-two-hour home passes, family members would have parties, not so much for me, but in general, I mingled with old friends, but things weren't the same. I felt the difference. My school friends had grown up. They had experienced life also. We all had grown into young adults, so to speak. My old friends, acquaintances, and family members were glad to see me. I was levelheaded. I carried myself in a more dignified manner. I've always liked to dress, even back in junior high.

Back when I started visiting home on a regular basis, *Afros* were still popular, so yes, I had my supernatural Afro. I had purchased clothes while on work release, so when I visited home, I would be sharp as a tack.

It was now wintertime. I was still coming and going from Gaston Correctional Center, working at Rauch Industries, and spending time at home. I was young and eager to be free again. God had allowed me a second chance. I didn't lose my life in the process. I wanted to make a positive difference as I reentered society.

As time passed as I worked, I was able to save money through work release, although I had to pay for living on the facility and support my daughter. The state saved money for me also.

Winter was coming to an end; now spring had sprung. It was now 1977. Good things were happening for me. I've always loved life. Spring passed like a breeze. It was now June 1, 1977. I turned nineteen years old. It had been twenty-five months since I was locked up and sentenced.

I had gone before the parole board many times while at Western Correctional Youth Institute, so I was familiar with the process. It was time for me to be evaluated for parole there at Gaston Correctional Center. I don't remember all that was said, but at this hearing, I had an opportunity to speak, so I did. I expressed my sincere gratitude to the parole board, stating that these two years in prison had given me the opportunity to build a solid foundation through my relationship with God, along with the structure and discipline that I had received for working to become a better person.

I don't know to this day who was in the parole hearing. I believe Captain Mears, who ran the facility at the time, was there. Nonetheless, after I finished speaking and several seconds passed, one of the men said a word or two and pronounced that they had approved me for parole. That meant that I could do the remainder of my sentence at home in Charlotte, North Carolina. Oh, what a happy day! That was sometime around the first of June. I was elated, man. I wanted to jump, run, or what have you. I wanted to cry, but I kept my composure.

After the parole hearing, I went back into the dome, where some of the men whom I had become close to were. They asked, "How did things go?"

I told them that I had made parole. They were happy and sad at the same time. We had spent a year together at Gaston Correctional

Center. We had laughed at each other, protected one another, and we were family, as it were. I still remember some of the guys today. I met some good people within my two years and one month of being in prison. I can honestly say, God being my witness, I don't have any regrets.

It would be several days before I was released. During that time, I made sure that I continued to stay the course. If memory serves me right, I was released on Friday, June 17, 1977. The same day, on October 17, 1975, on Friday, I entered the prison system—so ironic. The early afternoon on June 17, I was asked to come to the office, along with my belongings, clothes, etc. I entered the office at the correctional center. Captain Mears smiled and shook my hand and said that it had been a pleasure knowing me. He then introduced me to my parole officer. Massey was his name. He was a kind gentleman. He and I got into his state vehicle with my possessions in tow and drove out of the correctional center's parking lot for the last time.

On our way to Charlotte, Massey and I talked about many things—conditions of my parole, what my plans were now that I was back in Charlotte. As part of my parole, I had to report to my parole officer on a monthly basis and keep a place to live. I also was required to be employed—accountability, it's called.

CHAPTER 11

BACK AT HOME

We got into Charlotte and drove up to 920 Parkwood Avenue. Yes, I was back at home with Mom. As Massey and I departed, I finally had a chance to browse around the old neighborhood. Things were different. Twenty-five months had passed by. I was starting a new life. I don't remember who was home when I arrived. I only know that it was a beautiful day in the neighborhood.

I was home now. I hadn't made any particular plans as of yet. I had to get back into the flow of life. Like I said earlier, life doesn't stop because a person is in prison or dies. The world keeps on turning, and it's up to you to get back on track.

While I was coming home for home visits, my daughter's mother and I had gotten back together and were spending more time together. She had graduated from Garinger High School just weeks before I came home. It was a new relationship, so to speak. Both of us had experienced life in other ways during the twenty-five months.

She had matured. She wasn't the little girl I knew from fifteen years old. I wasn't the immature boy from 1975. I was now a young adult.

As the days passed by, I began to venture out more and more. My friends from the neighborhood heard that I was home, so I would visit little by little. My best friend Tom lived several houses up the street from me, so I visited him first. His mother was home that day and welcomed me in. This was the first time that she had seen me in over two years. Tom's mother was like a second mom to me.

Before I went to prison, I had been messing around with another girl beside my daughter's mother. I don't remember how she got the news that I would be at Tom's house, but lo and behold, she and one of her girlfriends were there. She was very happy to see me. I had been locked up for over two years. You don't just jump into relationships overnight, so I pulled away that time. I hadn't been sexually active for a long time, so I worked on not getting caught up in the same routine as I had been years before. My daughter's mom and I had begun having an intimate relationship again, so I wanted this time around to be different.

Days passed by, and now I had moved back in with Mom. Things were not the same. I had to get used to Mom and my younger siblings all over again. My sister, who was a year and a half younger, had grown up also. She was about as wild as I was years before. We loved each other but had gone our separate ways from years earlier.

She had been doing whatever she wanted to do, but I was still Big Brother, and that wasn't going to happen on my watch. Little did I know my sister was out of control!

I had a little money saved up while on work release at Dallas, but it didn't sustain me long. I had to get a *job*. One thing back in the day, you could get a job any day. All you had to do was go get it. You would fill out the application, give it to the receptionist, sit your tail down, and wait. Most of the time, you would be interviewed on the spot.

Well, that's what I did. There was a company called Coal Manufacturing located not far from where we lived off of Central Avenue. A lot of older men whom I knew worked there. Some of them had worked there for years. There were old friends whom I went to school with who worked there, as well as several members from this one family I knew. I applied at Coal Manufacturing Company and was hired on the spot. Usually, the person hiring you would ask when you could start. I was eager to get back into the workforce, so I told him that I could start the next day.

Well, I went home and broke the news to Mom. She was happy for me. After all, her son was home. Back in the day, when you were working to build a better life for yourself, family members would lend a hand up. They wanted to see you succeed in life and would go out of their way to help you. That's the kind of family I had. My brother and sisters always had my back even with my crazy ways.

Now that I was employed, I needed a car. Yes, I needed transportation. My eldest sister, whom I adored, and my brother-in-law had a blue 1968 Dodge Dart with a white top sitting in their backyard just waiting for me.

Well, having worked out a deal, as I can recollect, he wanted $200 for it. We agreed, and I paid him fifty dollars down on it. He signed over the title into my name. I got insurance put on it, purchased a tag, and now I'm driving my own car. Just a little sidenote: back then, young people worked on doing things right. You learn how to drive, get your driver's license, get a car, and put insurance on the vehicle. I could never understand how you can be all right driving without a driver's license and no insurance.

My daughter's mom and I dated more. The relationship entered a more serious aspect. We started talking about marriage, which I wasn't ready for, having just being paroled probably a month or so, and of course, the promiscuous ways began surfacing again. I began messing around with the other young woman whom I had been involved with before prison, so talking about marriage wasn't a thing or conversation I needed at the time. My daughter's mom had an idea that I was seeing the other woman and thought that the affair would stop when we were married. I kind of agreed in principle. In August 1977, the fourteenth of that month, she and I were married, the biggest decision I had made in my life up until then, and the most costly one, if I may say.

With no real, clear plans and the other woman, the marriage was in trouble from the beginning. I was living at home with Mom, which meant now, my wife had to move in with me, along with my two-year-old daughter. I could barely support myself, let alone a family. Mom didn't mind, but I was a man now. I had to start looking for a place of my own. I was no longer in a structured environment.

This was real life. There were no officers telling me what time to get up, what time to go to bed, and where I had to be at a certain time of the day. I was it. It wasn't Kansas. Dorothy and Toto weren't there!

I started my new job at Coal Manufacturing Company sometime in July, so I was working now. I wasn't a big communicator in regard to telling my new wife what was on my mind. I just did what I thought was right, not taking in consideration what my wife thought or wanted. I was part of the baby-boomer era, meaning we men did things the way we wanted to do and didn't want to be questioned about it, which wasn't good. I made all of the decisions, and my wife didn't seem to care too much. We were staying with Mom, and Mom had some rules and regulations in her home. I had to respect my wife and take care of my daughter, and at the same time, I was looking for a place of my own.

As far as I can remember, we lived with Mom for about a year. I had begun the cheating again; this time, I was married. I wanted to do the right thing but didn't practice the self-control needed to make the marriage grow. Well, sadly enough, the woman I had been cheating with got pregnant. Man, this really hurt my wife. Two months into the marriage, and I was already back to some of my old habits.

Things were up and down. Mom did not like or approve of how I was treating my wife, Barbara, and wasn't afraid to let me know. She loved Barbara just as her own daughter and wasn't going to let me treat her any kind of way. This caused friction between Mom and me, and I started to stay away from home at times.

I reunited with an old friend of mine from junior high. He and I had become good friends at Eastway Junior High, so I would spend nights at his house. He lived with his mom also and had the freedom to come and go as he pleased. We were now young adults. Charlie was my first white friend, and he would always look out for me. He knew my wife, Barbara, and wanted the marriage to work.

After several months at Coal Manufacturing, I left that job and began working with Charlie, who worked for a man who did landscaping. Well, the year was coming to an end. The last six months of 1977 hadn't been exactly what I had expected. I was back and forth at Mom's house, seeing Barbara and my daughter only then. I wasn't a good husband, let alone a father.

Mom stepped up as she always did for her children. Mom allowed Barbara and my daughter to stay at her house even while I was running around with Charlie. I wasn't seeing the other woman as well. We entered 1978. I remember coming home New Year's night. Barbara would be glad to see me anytime I was home. It always bothered me, but she never said anything. I continued to live as if I was single, hanging out with Charlie. Barbara was patient, always there at Mom's house when I decided to come home.

Finally, in the late spring of 1978, I landed a job at Gifford Hill, a company not far from where we lived on Parkwood Avenue. I don't know how I heard about the job, but a lot of my neighborhood friends worked there, even my best friend Tom. I was excited to be working a full-time job again. I was back at Mom's now. Barbara had always held a job. She was employed with Belk Brothers Department Store in uptown Charlotte. She had been employed with Belk's since graduating from high school.

We were finally able to get our first apartment at the Difference Apartments, located on Tom Hunter Road. Things began to look up for Barbara and I. Both of us were working now. It was now the late spring. June was around the corner. I hadn't been seeing the other woman much, but on June 2, 1978, my second daughter was born. I didn't go see my newborn baby right away. I was working on my marriage as much as could be expected during that time. Barbara didn't put up with my stupidity for much longer and began to speak up. She left me at the apartment.

I was now twenty years old and still didn't have any clear plans for the future. I was kind of living each day as it came. Shortly after Barbara moved out of the apartment, I moved the other woman in with me, along with my new baby girl. Barbara turned into the incredible Hulk. She trashed my blue-and-white 1968 Dodge Dart's windows that day in front of the neighbors, who were standing around to see what was going on in the parking lot. I was too embarrassed to go out to confront her. After some time had passed, I decided to call the police to help calm her down. When the police arrived, she was allowed to get her belongings and leave. I've never liked drama, but I was creating this for myself.

As the months passed, I was forced to move back home with Mom—yes, dear old Mom. Barbara and I had gotten back together and tried to work things out in the marriage. I was still messing around with my second daughter's mother. However, this was beginning to wear thin. I had given my life to the Lord while in jail, so God would be dealing with me regarding my lifestyle. Sometimes, a hard head makes a soft behind, and I was getting my tail kicked. There were many challenges that I was confronted with in the first year that I was home from prison.

It was now the winter of 1978. I had started going back into the gym. I hadn't worked out in the weight room for some time, but it came naturally. I joined Queen's Gym, which was located uptown Charlotte, corner of Fourth and College Streets. If memory serves me right, Louie Queen was the owner. I started working out just about every day. This was now my home away from home. Barbara and I were getting along fairly well, and she knew where I was.

Louie and I became good friends while I was at that gym. Back then, just about all of the wrestlers, if not all, worked out at Queen's Gym. It was a good place for me to be. This is where I met some of the big-name wrestlers like Ric Flair, Ricky Steamboat, and big Tony Atlas. I was finally able to refocus again. After working out at Queen's Gym for a while, I began to start training for bodybuilding again. It came naturally. I didn't know anything about steroids or what they are called today, performance enhancing drugs. I only knew hard consistent work would get me to where I wanted to be.

Things were looking up for me. The godly foundation was beginning to surface once more. The structure and discipline began to arise within me. During the year that I had been home from prison, I had managed to put God on the back burner, so to speak. During the twenty-five months of being locked up, I had made time to read my Bible and spend time in prayer, but now I had allowed life to blind me to spiritual things.

While working out at Queen's Gym, I met a man named David Van Every. He was a good-natured man, always seeming to be going somewhere. One day, as we were passing by each other at Queen's Gym, for some reason, he gave me his home address and asked me to come by sometime.

I didn't know at the time, but David had become a born-again Christian. I didn't think any more about visiting at his home. Barbara and I were working on our marriage and needed some positive people in our lives. We were still living with my mom at the time. I never remembered Mom ever putting a demand on us to move out. She was always helping us in any way possible. As a matter of fact, Mom let my eldest daughter sleep with her the whole time that we stayed with her. Mom loved her granddaughter; they bonded and established a lifelong relationship.

I was still working off and on with my friend Charlie, not really having a solid income. At that time, I was driving an old car that Charlie allowed me to drive to meet him on jobsites.

One day, I thought about the address that David Van Every had given me and decided to give him a visit. The address was located on Providence and Queens Roads. As I crossed Providence Road to get onto Queens Road, I thought, *David had given me the wrong house number*, so I drove up and down Queens Road.

I passed by Dave's address several times and thought surely this big house with a canary-yellow Corvette and a brown Porsche couldn't belong to David. He was a simple man, and he wasn't flashy, so this couldn't be where he lived. Well, I decided I'd just go up to the door and knock. As I knocked on the big door, the gentleman who opened the door was none other than David Van Every.

He greeted me with a warm smile and invited me in. As I entered the house, his wife came into the foyer, and David introduced us. He called her name. "Sheshe, this is Horace."

Sheshe was a warmhearted lady. We talked and became acquainted with one another, and after a while, David invited me downstairs to show me his gym—yes, his gym! It was a really well-equipped gym. He even had a water cooler that dispensed Perrier bottled water, a carbonated mineral water. To this day, I never got used to drinking Perrier!

As we talked about bodybuilding and working out, Dave, as I became accustomed to calling him (later on Charles), asked me if I would be interested in training with him there at his home. I didn't hesitate to say, "Yes, I would love to. What an opportunity to really get into bodybuilding."

Dave and I became good friends during our days of working out together. I can't remember if I had competed in the Mr. Charlotte bodybuilding contest before I met Dave or afterward.

Nonetheless, I had found my niche. I was finally doing what I always wanted to do—bodybuilding. David mentioned earlier that he was going to be opening up his own gym, and he wanted me to be one of his instructors. Things were getting better at home also. Barbara and I were happy, and she was supporting me in my new life change.

As the King's Gym was being built, Dave and I, along with another best friend of his, continued to train at his home on Queens Road.

Dave was older than me and was like a big brother to me. I've always enjoyed being around real men, men who knew who they are. I never liked being around sissies or cowards. Dave was a strong, energetic man. I loved him like he was my own flesh and blood. He was a white man. I say this because the color of a man's skin never bothered me—it's the content of his character.

At this time of my life, I was still navigating the direction that I wanted to take. Sometimes when you don't have a plan of your own, you allow other people's plans to guide you. That's not always good.

Barbara and I were still working on our marriage. I was staying at home more and more. We even found the time to take trips together on weekends. Dave was a big influence on me. I loved the way he treated his wife, Sheshe. Being around people with morals can sometimes rub off on you.

The winter of 1978 had ended. It was the latter part of spring. Again, June 1 was quickly approaching, and I was about to turn twenty-one years old. I was going on two years since being out of prison. I was doing good and making better choices. I was more focused on my family now.

Well, King's Gym finally opened in June 1979. It was the best gym on this side of the Mississippi River. I started full-time at King's Gym. It was a beautiful gym in terms of how Dave had things decorated, carpeted, and painted, and all of the equipment was the best. The locker rooms, wet rooms, showers—everything was of high quality. We even had a fully operated juice bar. Man, I was finally back in Kansas!

Now I was able to move out of the house with Mom. Barbara and I were able to get our own place. We moved into a two-bedroom apartment in Cobblestone Apartments located on Idlewild and Monroe Roads. At the time, shag carpet was a big thing. We were able to buy furniture for the entire apartment.

Barbara was employed at Belk's Department Store, so we brought our front-room furniture from Belk's, and yes, we got a discount! This was our second apartment together, so I made sure that we weren't going to make the same mistakes as before.

Barbara and I also celebrated the birth of our second daughter. I now had three daughters, including one I had with the other woman. I was a little more mature now and in a good place in life, mentally as well as financially. Having two incomes can do a lot for beginning families.

My second daughter with Barbara was my joy. I loved my two older children also. I was more stable now and could come home and enjoy my two daughters. My baby girl started walking at nine months old and could also climb up and down the stairs. Girls can often steal their father's heart like no one else.

I welcomed the home environment and looked forward to being home in the evenings. I worked the first shift at the gym and could be home at night. Life was grand, but I still hadn't started going to church.

I never was a person who did drugs or who loved alcohol. My friends and family would drink whiskey and beer, and because I was around my friends, usually white men, I would smoke pot. They would have the real thing. I would occasionally drink beer or Bacardi Rum and Coca-Cola. I guess you would have called me a social drinker. I loved working out in the weight room, so drinking and smoking wasn't really my thing or a habit.

As the months passed, I began to enjoy where I was in life—family, job, good friends, so to speak. God had given me so many chances. As I look back, God had been better to me than I had been to myself.

Two years had now come and gone. I had finally gotten back into the flow of life. I had matured in my dealings with people in society as a whole. I was happy most of the time when things were going my way, but could fly off the handle at the drop of a dime. My anger would cause me problems all through my youth and adult life.

CHAPTER 12

ENJOYING BODY BUILDING

Barbara and I were enjoying the social life as well. Working at King's Gym afforded me opportunities to meet celebrities, big-time athletes, and businessmen—people from all walks of life. I met then-renowned Jim Bakker, the Levine family, and Dexter Yager. Dave even had the greatest bodybuilder I know to this day, Arnold Schwarzenegger, come to Charlotte for our grand opening. Arnold and I hit it off from the first moment that Dave introduced us. I loved people and still do, so it's never been a problem having new people in my life.

I had started training for the Mr. America contest that would be hosted in New York City come September 1979, so I was working out just about every day. I stayed in shape all through the year, so it was fairly easy for me to get ready for a contest in no time.

Members at the gym knew that I was going to compete in the WBBG Mr. America contest. Several of them became my sponsors. I stayed on the straight and narrow for the most part but then started my old ways again. Barbara and I were getting along so well at home. Life was good. I was enjoying my job at the gym. Dave was a good boss man to work for. He always supported Barbara and I.

I hadn't seen my second daughter's mom for a long time, but I would think about my daughter. Barbara hadn't accepted the fact that I had a child by the other woman. I had been dating the both of them before we were married. It had been two years now, and my second daughter's mom, Sheila, had moved on also. When I did come around, I could sense the difference in the relationship. Hey, who in their right mind hangs around, waiting on a married man who has a family, and pops up when he feels like it?

Sheila had been seeing other men also and had another daughter during that time. I thought that the child was mine and was willing to accept the responsibility for the child, but Sheila informed me that the child was not mine and that I could move on. I was hurt when she told me the news, but as time passed, I had a chance to meet the gentleman who fathered the child.

After I started working at King's Gym, I would hang around the people I met while they worked out at the gym. Some of the guys were like family. King's Gym had a positive effect on my life. It gave me a chance to meet new people from all walks of life.

Well, September rolled around, and it was time for me to prepare for the trip to New York City. I would be competing in the 1979 World Body Building Guild (WBBG) Mr. America contest. It would be my first professional competition. I had won my first amateur competition several months earlier, Mr. Charlotte, a regional or citywide contest. That contest really gave me the confidence throughout the time of my days preparing for the Mr. America competition.

I was pretty much a newcomer into the sport and was naive in many ways. Again, I wasn't familiar with the steroid usage, so I didn't concern myself with the process. I did study and read about the results that you could obtain from using them, but the side effects weren't something that I wanted to deal with, so I competed naturally. I knew how to train without drugs.

Steroids gave you bulk, size, density, striations, and so on if used correctly, and monitored by a physician, you can achieve tremendous results. I just didn't want to go that route. Many of the men in the gym did.

One of my sponsor's sons and I flew into New York on the Friday before the Mr. America contest. The competition was on Saturday. This was my second visit to New York. The first time I visited was a year before when I drove up with Louie Queen, owner of Queen's Gym. At that first visit, the World Body Building Guild was inducting Clint Eastwood into the bodybuilders' Hall of Fame. It was a formal event, and Louie and I dressed the part.

This may have been when David Van Every told me that he was building King's Gym. He also attended the event. As my sponsor's son Stephen and I arrived in New York by airplane, we were carried to our hotel by cab. For the rest of our stay, we travel by subway.

The Mr. America competition was held at the historic Walt Whitman High School, where the old sitcom *Room 222* was filmed. I've always enjoyed visiting New York. Back in the '70s, the boroughs were just that rough! The city has come a long way since then.

Saturday came, and we caught the subway to Walt Whitman High. There were people already lined up to get into the auditorium. As we stood in line, we met Tony Atlas and another bodybuilder from King's Gym. They were competing in the Mr. America also. The one gentleman was competing as a teenager. Tony and I would be competing against each other. He would be competing as a heavyweight and I as a middleweight. As we entered the auditorium, we were directed backstage, where we would dress out, pump up, and grease down.

Bodybuilders stayed shaved. We didn't know when we would be invited to do an exhibition. We sat and watched the younger competitors through their competition, and then came my time. I've never been intimidated by anyone, let alone another man, so I got ready backstage with other men in my group. I've always had symmetry while competing, so the confidence would be there. I always possessed well-developed abs, along with the other body parts that would get me noticed.

Each man would be called out individually to perform his routine, greased down, and pumped up, posing in front of the judges. It was a high like no other, the audience cheering you on, clapping, screaming, everyone enjoying and appreciating the hard work that had gotten us to this point.

Stage presence was important, and I loved everything about it. It was a dream come true. Well, when one of the heavyweight competitors didn't win his weight class and stormed off of the stage in anger and eventually out of the auditorium. His actions disrupted the entire contest. To this day, I don't *remember* how everything else ended. It was just several years ago that I was browsing through the Internet and looked up WBBG, and there was Horace Ivey finishing third in the middle-class competition. It's there in history.

If memory serves me right, my sponsor's son Stephen and I left the auditorium. It was later that Saturday night, September 1979. It was cold, and I hadn't dressed accordingly. I only had on the King's Gym T-shirt. I wasn't familiar with New York's cold weather in September.

We caught the subway back to our hotel. In our ignorance, we got off the subway several blocks before we should have and had to walk a couple more blocks to our hotel. New York blocks are longer than normal, so we experienced the cold, long walk for our lack of knowledge.

Well, the next day, Sunday morning, after breakfast, we made our way to the airport, heading back to Charlotte. The trip wasn't as enjoyable as it could have been because I had taken along an extra person who shouldn't have gone with us.

I had to be back at work the following Monday morning. Everyone was asking about how things went and where I placed in my weight class. At the time, I didn't really know. Things settled down and got back to normalcy. I was back at home. I didn't talk to Barbara much about my trip to New York. I was back at King's Gym. I was now twenty-one years old and still didn't have a clear picture or plan for what was next for me and my young family.

I hadn't learned how to pray and make decisions based on where I was at the time. As the weeks and months passed, I started slipping back into the cheating again. Sheila had moved on, but I would just pop up from nowhere. Sheila was living with her family, and they knew that I was married and didn't take too kindly to my coming around.

Sometimes you can't put everything on the devil or on someone else. You have to take a look in the mirror! I was my worst enemy. It seemed that I would take one step forward and two steps backward. This had been going on for the last two years. I was making these bad decisions again, coming home anytime in the mornings, not respecting Barbara.

Trouble was brewing at my job. I was no longer getting along with my boss David. Things begin to fall apart after about a year of this foolishness. The cheating, the disrespect of my boss man Dave, who was also my friend. He called me into his office, along with the gym manager, and informed me that I was fired.

I knew that this had to happen but wasn't prepared financially. I wasn't saving any money. Every dollar that came in went out just as fast. We were living from paycheck to paycheck with no plans and no clear directions. The news of my firing was devastating. It was my lifeline. I depended on this monthly income.

I didn't acknowledge how dependent I was on my job. It was everything at the time. A $235-a-month rent payment, furniture, lights, insurance, etc. As Dave broke the news of my firing, I couldn't do anything but cry. Tears ran down my cheeks. I hugged Dave because not only had I lost my job, but I had lost a good friend. There is a saying that goes like this: be careful how you treat people as you climb up the ladder because you will pass them again coming down.

We finally lost our apartment, bills piled up, and things fell apart. It was my own doing. It wasn't my wife, Barbara. It wasn't my employer. It was Horace Ivey. I had to own up to it. Barbara moved in with my brother and his wife. I stayed at the apartment just long enough to pack up our belongings.

I got a job at the Family Dollar warehouse out on Monroe Road for a brief while. Again not having any plans, I eventually moved in with Barbara and my daughters at my brother's home. It was now the winter of 1980. I was in and out, still doing whatever I pleased, cheating, hanging out with some old friends and family, and just living a reckless life.

The year was coming to an end. Barbara and I were living with my brother, his wife, and their two boys. I had two young daughters also. Family will always make room for you even when things weren't going well for them. That is how family loved each other!

I believe that one of the biggest changes in my life up to that time is when the woman I had been cheating with, Sheila, had gotten an apartment of her own, where at times I would just pop up. One morning, I came by her apartment unannounced and found the keys in the back door. I opened up the door quietly and walked up the stairs and caught Sheila and her second daughter's father lying across the bed, just having a conversation. They had on clothes, nothing nasty. They were just talking.

As I entered the bedroom, Sheila became outraged and asked me to leave immediately. The gentleman got up, and we introduced ourselves. There was no argument or fussing. We simply were surprised. After several minutes passed, he said that he would leave because he didn't know that I was still in a relationship with Sheila, which I really wasn't. He finally left, and after packing up several items that I had there at her apartment, I left also. That was the last time that I ever went to her home again.

It was the beginning of 1981; after three to four years of marriage, I started to think about getting involved in church. I hadn't been a good example of anything close to being a Christian up until then. I really needed a real change in my life, so I began attending church with Barbara at her home church. We were still living with my brother and his family at the time.

Barbara was always ready to do whatever it took to make things work for the good of the family. While living with our family, Barbara got a job at the old Cannon Mills in Kannapolis, North Carolina. People from Charlotte drove from the two points all the time.

Barbara worked second shift. That meant I could be there to make sure my elder daughter and my baby girl were taken care of. After a few weeks of working at Cannon Mills, I decided to join Barbara at the mill on second shift. We would drop off the girls at Mom's before going to work.

Working together allowed us to get back on the fast track to being in our own place again. It was Christmastime 1980. Jim Bakker's PTL Club was experiencing growth all over the globe at this time. I started watching the Christian-based television show on a daily basis. Jim and Tammy were so encouraging, along with Uncle Henry.

My sister-in-law also started watching the show. PTL had people from all walks of life on the show each day. I looked forward to watching *The Jim Bakker Show* every day.

Several months prior to working at Cannon Mills, I had a divine encounter with God while visiting Barbara's home church. I guess God knew that I was finally serious enough to help me make the choice of serving him completely. After that encounter, I begin to seek God more and more. I even began to read my Bible again, something that I hadn't been doing for quite some time.

After joining Barbara at Cannon Mills on second shift, I was introduced to a man. We call him Reverend Brown. He was a highly spiritual man. He and I became close friends right from the beginning. He was like a brother from another mother.

GOING TO CHURCH

As I began to attend church, I surrounded myself with other church-going families who were married and raising young children. I wasn't a man of godly integrity at the time and was just navigating my way through this new life of Christianity. I was a young adult and had a strong personality. I really had just begun to enter into life as a normal person, meaning a lot of the baggage that I had lived with for years was finally beginning to fall off.

I was treating Barbara and my children with more and more compassion. I even grew to love others as I learned to love myself. I knew something had changed within my very being. God was becoming more and more real to me. Thank God for his unending love for me.

After working at Cannon Mills for several months, Barbara and I were able to get our own place again! In February 1981, we moved out of my brother's home into our third apartment at the time, Barrington Oaks Apartments off the Plaza Extension. Again, this is not a religious narrative, but there is no way that I can leave out God, the Creator, the master builder, the life source of all creation that exists.

Good things would happen at this point of my life, my new life in Christ. God was allowing me to meet some really good people in the church. I've always been a little naive when it came to meeting people. I've always wanted to trust and be free with family as well as strangers. God put a new heart of gold inside my spirit. I wanted everyone to know that I was a changed man.

I quickly found that not everyone celebrated my new Christian life, like I thought they would. There were haters in my family as well as in the church. At that point, I didn't have a godly mentor, a man who would help me grow into a godly husband and father, so I allowed God through his Holy Spirit to teach me through the study of the Bible and spending time with him in prayer and meditation. The Bible literally became my best friend as I sought God's guidance. He led me to a few men who had been in Christian ministry several years before me. Being around those men who knew how to treat their spouses helped me change the way I treated Barbara.

As I continued to grow spiritually and mentally, I became more aware of having plans, goals, dreams, and aspirations; components I never envisioned at the time.

Even from childhood, I knew that there was much more to living than just a day. The world is huge—so much to look forward to, so much to see, places to go, so much to achieve. I would always be ready for bigger and better challenges. Life is wonderful!

In February 1982 or thereabouts, I was introduced to an evangelist who was on fire for God. His excitement for seeing people come to God got me eager to see other lives changed and transformed by God's Holy Spirit. When I first met him, he was meeting at one of Charlotte's hotels. His services were held on Sunday nights, giving me and my family an opportunity to attend our church on Sunday mornings. After several months of meeting at the hotel, the evangelist announced that he was starting his own church. With no hesitation, Barbara and I joined with him and became some of his first members.

We helped with about every facet of the ministry. Carpeting, cleaning commodes—you name it, we would do it. This was an exciting time in my spiritual growth, as well as in developing as a godly man. I was given responsibilities because of my faithfulness and loyalty to God and the man of God. I eventually became an elder in the church. I've always sensed a call of God on my life but didn't know how to go about preparing myself to be used of God.

This evangelist helped point me in the right direction, but it wasn't without trial and error. Oh, yes, I made some immature decisions!

One of the best things that I've done was to engross myself into God's Word, the Bible. I became a student and a sponge for the Word of God, taking advantage of every opportunity to get involved in any Bible class. While attending this church, the evangelist, now pastor, started a Bible Institute, where I became a student and sometimes instructor. I loved this man and his family. We became family, and for the first time in my life, I began to experience what true love was like in God's family.

At this time in my young adult life, I was sensitive and could be at times emotionally unstable. I had to learn how to control my emotions, something that I will be working on until the day that I leave this world!

I was experiencing growth in about all areas of life. My faith in God was really surfacing as I depended on him more and more. As the church started to grow, more families joined the church. It was beautiful seeing young adults come to God.

After about a year or more, 1981, Barbara and I discovered that she was pregnant. I already had three daughters and was really excited about having a son. Well, after about nine months, Barbara finally delivered a baby boy on July 17, 1982. Weighing over eight pounds, we named him Horace Leon Ivey Junior. He became an added joy to my life. He was a good baby.

We stayed at this church for maybe a year and a half and experienced some much-needed spiritual growth. After seeking God's direction, it was time to move on. I had a sister who also become a Christian and was excited about her new life in Christ. She would tell me about a preacher who was on a particular radio station in the Charlotte, North Carolina, area and encouraged me to listen to his broadcast. At that time, I had come out of the denominational churches and wanted more freedom to worship God and hear the Bible taught in its entirety.

I had already started listening to some of the greatest Bible teachers at the time on television and radio, even on tapes. I was hungry for God's Word like never before. The more of God's Word

I got, the more freedom from my old life I experienced. Sin was no longer controlling me like before.

As I started listening to that preacher and found out where he was holding services, I finally attended one of his Sunday-morning services, and to my amazement, up until that time, I had never heard the Word of God taught with so much simplicity, yet it was profound in scope. There were hundreds of people already attending this church, and because I was so eager to be around this kind of atmosphere, I quickly became a member.

I met people from all around Charlotte and the surrounding areas. The pastor was dynamic and knowledgeable pertaining to delivering God's Word to his people. Barbara welcomed the tremendous transformation that was taking place in my life. Barbara had been raised up in church but hadn't accepted Christ as her Lord and Savior.

After I got serious with God, Barbara really gave her life to Christ and became a born-again Christian. Our home became a light to not only our church family but to my biological family as well. My mom, brothers, and sisters saw the change that God had made in my life. All of my childhood friends and neighbors heard about the new man who I had become. I hadn't arrived, but I was headed in the right direction. I welcomed the change!

At the time, I didn't know what I was supposed to be doing in regard to working on a particular job or occupation, so I took on various jobs to provide for my family. I drove trucks, sold gym equipment, worked in gymnasiums again. I was satisfied just knowing that Barbara and my children were being taken care of. I wanted to be wherever God wanted me to be.

Being a member of our new church allowed Barbara and I a chance to meet with other couples who also had children our children's age. Man, things were happening so well, I thought that I had died and was in heaven!

This was between 1983 and 1984. My children were young, and I was spending most of my time with them. My children were my lifeline. I simply adored them. There wasn't anywhere that I went that they couldn't come along.

One of my biggest challenges was being stable on my jobs. I knew my potential to learn and lead, so I wasn't content with just allowing people to control my livelihood. Most of the time, when you are working for someone, a business or corporation, you become a number, someone hired to fill a volume. You are handed a company handbook and expected to perform your duties, get along with your colleagues, come to work, clock in, do what you are told, smile, and pretend you are in with what the company stands for, then you go home. Well, that's not how I function. I've got to know that I'm making a difference and that I'm contributing. I've got to know there is a rainbow at the end of the tunnel. I don't like wasting time!

I had a family to support, four children now. I was struggling financially. Even though Barbara worked, it seemed that there was never enough money coming into the house. I wasn't a lazy man and would take on any kind of extra work. My days of being a criminal were over. I wasn't squeaky clean, but I wasn't ever spending time in jail again.

I've always wanted to attend college. I thought about it all the time, but having a young family to support, I just couldn't seem to find the time. It takes money to raise children and lots of it! When there's a man, father, in the home, the woman or children shouldn't know that there is not enough. He should have the ability to make things look as though everything will be all right, and that is what I usually did.

Several years had passed, and I was still enjoying my new life as a Christian. It was the spring of 1984. My son was now two years old. I couldn't wait to be with him. I looked forward to teaching him sports, teaching him how to be strong in every area of his life. I talked to him about God even though he was only two years old. He loved being with his dad.

God had blessed me with friends who owned homes at Myrtle Beach and condos in the Banner Elk mountains, so they would allow me and my family to stay at their places. No one occupied the properties, so I could call and ask to use the beach condo or stay at the condo in Banner Elk. Barbara and the children loved getting away from home. I enjoyed being with my family.

In the spring of 1984, I got a job at a gym equipment company on the Plaza Road as a truck driver. I would deliver gym equipment and assemble the equipment for gyms, businesses, and homes all over the country. I loved traveling up and down the highways. What freedom, what joy it was setting up gyms all over America. I had spent most of my life in the gym, and now I was getting paid to do what I loved.

One of the most rewarding things about the job was that I was able to take my son along with me. He hadn't started day care or preschool at the time. We went everywhere, delivering gym equipment, staying in hotels, eating, and swimming in the hotel pools. If we stayed overnight, I made sure to read my Bible in front of him. I've always wanted my children to know God.

Well, about a year of traveling from city to city, state to state, it was time for my son to go to school. I had become use to riding with him. I missed him tremendously.

After working in the gym industry for so many years, in the spring of 1985, I left the gym equipment company and started my own business, personalized fitness training. I had clients from all walks of life—rich, middle class, professionals, businessmen, women, and former athletes. You name them, I trained them! The work was fulfilling. I loved working with my clients. Some of them became friends.

I enjoyed the fitness training. For one, it gave me the privilege of helping people achieve personal goals and their physical development. Although man is a threefold being, it is very important that we pay attention to our bodies. Being self-employed allowed me also to spend more time with my family. My children were in elementary school, and I needed to be there for them. I attended the PTA meetings, volunteered for school projects, ate lunch with my children, supported the teachers, and yes, I supported my children. If they got out of line, they knew Dad would be there and vice versa. If the teacher got out of line, I would have a conference with them.

My third daughter, who was strong-willed even as a child, would challenge her teachers. She wasn't disruptive or anything like that. She knew who she was and what she wanted. Hey, sounds like someone I know! I can truly say even to this day, I loved and enjoyed being a father. I have no regrets.

We had moved into a house by now into the Bridlewood section of the plaza area. The apartment life had gotten too confined for raising my children. I couldn't allow them to just hang out in certain parts of the neighborhood. Although we had family living all around us, I was very protective of my children.

Like I've said earlier, I loved training my clients, and most, if not all of them, achieved their intended goals. While training in the gym one day, I met a gentleman, whose wife was the secretary for the original Charlotte Hornets. The gentleman informed me that the Charlotte Hornets was looking for a strength-and-conditioning coach. My name was passed on to his wife. This was an opportunity for me to move up into a position that I had prepared for most of my young adult life.

I quickly set up an appointment to meet with Coach Dick Harter through his secretary. Sometimes being in the right place at the right time can open up the right doors. As I sat in the office of Dick Harter, I was able to meet the assistant coach as well, Gene Little. He was just passing by, and we introduced ourselves. Coach Little had a good mannerism about himself. I liked him instantly.

After several minutes had passed, Coach Harter entered the office, and his secretary introduced us. The meeting wasn't long and drawn out, but he told me what he was looking for and asked me if I would be interested in an interim position for right now. I believe this was his first head-coaching position, so I understood his reasoning. He asked me to come to the training sessions and get to know the players and how things were set up—the practices, warm-ups, stretching in general—what was required for the strength and condition coach position.

It wasn't a problem at first because I still had my business as a fitness trainer. This was at the peak of Michael Jordan's career, so I welcomed the opportunity of being around professional basketball players. I was also supplying supplements to some of the players. At the time, several of the Hornets was wearing Converse shoes and apparel, so I was able to visit the Converse warehouse with the likes of Muggsy Bogues, who gave me the nickname Herc, short for Hercules. I got my first pair of Converse basketball shoes and warm-ups hanging out with the players. Some of the players would have side gigs and would invite us, players and coaches, to join them at certain eating places. This offered me the opportunities for free meals!

I had been given an ID card so I could get free stuff at times. I loved being at the game-day shootarounds. These were professional basketball players, some of whom I watched as college players. I got to know some of them personally. Others, I would keep the business side with them. I looked forward to the Chicago Bulls coming to Charlotte to play the Hornets. Having been a North Carolina Tar Heels fan all my life and being a Michael Jordan fan, I relished getting the chance to see the Bulls shootaround. After the Chicago Bulls shootaround, there would be a media frenzy to get an interview with none other than Michael Jordan.

Now mind you, this was not a paid position as the interim strength-and-conditioning coach. Coach Harter and I agreed only in principle regarding the position. He didn't promise me anything! I was just happy to get the opportunity to hang out with the players. I did this for several weeks but found it to be more than I wanted to put into the waiting period, so I kind of drifted out of the picture, so to speak.

I continued to do the personalized fitness training for a short time after pursuing the Hornets strength-and-conditioning position. I was always ready and willing to move on to bigger and better ambitions in life. My family always took center stage no matter what other path or venture that I was pursuing.

After the winter of 1986, I felt like the Lord was calling me to ministry. I didn't know exactly where or when. The pastor of the church that I had joined three years earlier started having monthly meetings with those of us who believed that we were called into the Christian ministry. I wasn't raised in church, so I didn't have a clue on how you prepared to enter the ministry. My new pastor was seasoned in this area, so I was excited about learning church protocol, the official procedure of rules governing the affairs of the church.

I continued working in the health-and-fitness arena for several more years, and in 1989, I closed down the fitness training business. I still had a family to support! I took on various jobs to keep food on the table, as it were. After about a year and a half of wrestling with the desire of going into full-time ministry through prayer and meeting with my pastor, I informed Barbara that I had felt a strong leading to go into ministry on a full-time basis. Barbara was always willing to support me in any way she could and never complained.

In the winter of 1990, I prepared myself to *seek* where I believed God wanted me to be. For several months, I prayed and sought God's direction for where I should go regarding starting the church. After the months of prayer, I talked to Barbara about visiting Greensboro, North Carolina. The family and I loved spending time together wherever we went. Whether visiting the beach, mountains, or anywhere else, it didn't matter; we loved being together. We visited Greensboro several times before making the final decision.

Well, in the early spring, I believe in 1991, I moved my family to Greensboro, North Carolina. What a leap of faith, along with a little backbone. I had said goodbye to our friends back at our home church. We had some supporters, and as always, there were haters. It's always amazing to me that some people don't have a vision for their own lives and don't want you to envision better things for you and your family! Just a little sidenote: when I'm making plans for my family, I never ever discuss my plans with my biological family. Every family member should have and live their own lives. Yes, I believe in family, but at the same time, there has to be a cutting of the umbilical cord.

The move to Greensboro, North Carolina, brought Barbara, the children and I even closer. I've always been protective of my family, and so it was now. Before we moved to Greensboro, I had gotten a job at the United States Postal Service, so I was able to transfer my employment to Greensboro. We had moved into an apartment off of Holden Road and Church Street. It was there that I started having Bible studies at our apartment. We would invite neighbors, coworkers—whomever we met. I was so glad to be doing what I believe the Lord had called me to do. Having left my family, friends, and my familiar surroundings back in Charlotte, I had to depend solely on the Lord. It wasn't always easy, to tell the truth!

As I've mentioned before, it costs money to raise children, so it was now. Barbara had been employed with Belk's back in Charlotte and was able to land a retail job in Greensboro. We continued Bible study for several months, and after visiting several places around Greensboro, I found a building located on Market Street in Greensboro. I worked at the post office right up the street from the building that I eventually rented.

In July 1991, we started Faith Christian Center with none other than the five of us, meaning Barbara, my three children, and I. Yes, I had four children at the time, but my second eldest daughter never lived with me, just another sidenote.

The company representative that we rented the building from was always so supportive of the church, especially the woman who actually met with me the day that I signed the lease. I was always aware of endeavoring to represent the Lord in my everyday life. I was no longer sitting under the leadership of my pastor, so to speak. But I kept in contact with him often. It seemed as if he'd be there with me in about every decision that I made. Having spent the last eight years under my pastor's tutelage, I had observed and learned somewhat and became familiar with the functioning of church matters.

I'll say this: don't ever think that you've arrived in maturity in life, walking behind someone else's shoes. One size does not fit all. As we mature, you will learn that you are a unique individual. You have a totally different DNA than anyone on Planet Earth, and until you learn this, you will never complete your life goals, dreams, aspirations, plans, or vision. It's good to have a mentor but even better to have divine leadership from the inside out. No person, place, thing, or idea can complete you other than the man himself, the man Christ Jesus.

I've endeavored as much as possible not to make this a religious narrative, but hey, you have to make that decision. As we started the Bible studies in our new building, weeks passed by. It was just my four and no more. I prayed and taught the Word. I was consistent and persistent, knowing surely that the Lord had called me to this place. In life, you can't be moved by what you see. Your feelings and emotions will, most of the time, cripple you and stop God's plan and direction for your life. You cannot—you must not—allow fear to stop the flow of God's heavenly plan for your life.

Well, after several weeks of preaching to the choir that is my wife and children, people started visiting the church. After a while, we had our first members. The "Lord began adding daily such as needed to be saved." It was simply God doing what he does best.

I met a preacher while in the ministry who said this: "All you have to do is rent a building and put up a sign, and people will come." And I quote, "I would hope and pray that it's more to church than that."

It was 1991. As the Lord began adding to the church, I remained steadfast in communicating the gospel to those who joined Faith Christian Center. The little building or space we were renting didn't allow us much activity, but we made it work for such a time as we needed. I did have an office on the second floor of the same building where I conducted church business. We eventually fixed up the little space that we conducted our weekly services.

As the church began to grow, I knew that I had to find a bigger building to hold our weekly services. I started looking for another building throughout the city of Greensboro, North Carolina.

After about two years at the Market Street location, I found a building on the other side of town. At the time of writing this book, I can't remember the address. I met with the owners of the building and was able to lease the new location. It was a building that stood by itself. Now we could enjoy the freedom to do more in terms of ministry. The building needed some renovations, so I set out to do the improvements.

The congregation was excited about our new location. They were eager to give and support the project. Our color was royal blue and a slightly pinkish color. The carpet, which was new, accented each other. I added an extra wall to the entrance of the building to give privacy to my office, children's area, and our restrooms. The chairs were royal blue also, which I and one of the men in the church drove to Rome, Georgia, to pick up. The interior of the building was absolutely beautiful. One of the men who worked at a sign company made a sign for the building, reading, "Faith Christian Center." We experienced some growth and were excited. God was using me to fulfill the vision that he had long ago birthed in my spirit.

In this section of the book, as we move forward, I'm going to open myself up to a period in my personal life that was probably the most shameful and embarrassing time of my adult life, a time that most likely changed the course of my future, family, ministry, and yes, other people's lives.

You see, when you are in a place of leadership, people look to you for just that, to "lead the ship." When you are placed in a place of authority either by man or God or maybe succeed in business, it is very, very important that you also develop godly character because you are responsible not only to lead but to exemplify morality and integrity for the people whom you are *leading* or who are looking up to you. This is something that's required of you by necessity. And as you go further up in life, your morality and character, or lack of, will be exposed.

Generally speaking, I don't believe that anyone in their right mind ever set out to hurt people or themselves. It can be through just not being taught at an early age or just not having been trained properly or just plain ignorance. Either way, there's no excuse people's lives are at stake.

After about four years as pastor of the church, as we grew and became a church family, people from all around the surrounding area started attending our church. It was a refreshing and fulfilling time in my life. Barbara and the children were happy. Couples were joining the church who had children, so my children welcomed the increase. Several Universities were located nearby, so we attracted college students as well.

I preached and taught biblical principles, getting to know God on a more personal basis, thereby working on increasing our faith in God's integrity and his Word. I loved my congregation and was always there for them, whether counseling, spending time with each family, fellowshipping with the men on the basketball court, conducting marriage classes, and meeting with the singles. Whatever it was, it was a privilege and honor to lead and pastor God's people.

Now let me make this "strong point," men! There are always going to be more women than men. Sidenote: our relationship with our mothers, sisters, our women cousins, and the young ladies in our neighborhoods and schools will be indicative or will serve as a sign of our future relationships with our girlfriends, wives, and other females. For the record, I did not have a good relationship with my biological mother and had hardly any respect for her in the early stage of my life. Now that changed when I became a born-again Christian over a period of time. It was a process.

Yes, sometimes as life progresses, as men and women, we begin to make biological changes. These changes happen to all of us if we live long enough. We go from being twenty-five years old to thirty-five. Each growth stage brings on, as it were, new challenges in our maturation phase of life. For women, you call this period going through the change of life, where men experience the same biological changes. Little do most men know, we call this period midlife crisis, where our bodies and minds are no longer as young as they once were. It's at this period of life, if we are not aware or informed, that we can do some crazy things. This biological and mental change can and will likely happen at different stages of adult life, some earlier than others.

I was pastoring at a time when things were happening in my personal life that I truly didn't understand. It's easy to ignore stuff that you have to deal with when you are constantly trying to help others. Well, this happened to me. I was so caught up with helping everyone around me that I forgot to minister to myself. My biological time clock was ticking, but I didn't have the knowledge or the wherewithal to recognize what was happening to me. Barbara and I were getting along well, the ministry was going well, and things were looking up.

Sometimes when you are helping people and giving advice, you can get too personally involved with the situation and people you are endeavoring to help. I got involved with a young lady in my church, helping her to get out of her living situation with a woman she was renting from while she attended one of the universities in Greensboro, North Carolina. We will call her Maria. I was working out at a gym one day and noticed on the information board that there was a woman who had a room for rent. At the time, Maria was a member of my church. I didn't pay much attention, so I just casually wrote down the woman's name and phone number and gave it to Maria. Several weeks into getting or renting this room from the woman, Maria would call me up and say that the woman had mental issues.

Remember, it was I who had given Maria the woman's phone number, so being the person responsible for having gotten Maria in this situation, I was somewhat responsible for helping get her out. I had a meeting with Barbara and the children at home at the kitchen table and talked with them about Maria's possibly moving in with us until she found other living arrangements. As we talked, I could see that Barbara didn't want anything to do with Maria's coming to stay with us, not even one day. The children knew Maria from church and had somewhat of a relationship with her.

I can still see Barbara's expression to this day. She was not in agreement with this decision to move Maria into our home. After convincing the family that it was only for a short period, against my better judgment, Maria moved in with us.

It turned out to be a fatal decision! It was then that my whole life turned upside down. I had no plan for or idea that things would turn out the way that they did. Wow!

Sometimes when we are facing temptations, things that come upon us suddenly, we may have to run, just leaving everything behind, just like Joseph did in Genesis 39:11–12. He literally ran from Potiphar's wife. Joseph left the garment that he was wearing. In James 1:13–15, the Bible tells us, "Let no man say when he is tempted, I am tempted of God." At the time, Barbara was traveling back and forth to Charlotte. She was attending college at our church's school of ministry. I want to make it absolutely clear to my readers. God be my judge, I never planned or dreamed that I would be involved or caught up in an affair with this young woman in such a way that I did!

It was the ending of 1993. The relationship or the affair got heated up. It was several months. Things in my life, home, and church started breaking down. I no longer was in control of my senses, as it were. I went after this young woman with no thought or concern regarding the consequences that I would cause my family, church, or my reputation as a pastor, let alone a man.

I had no idea that it would affect not only Maria but her family as well. The choice that I made in entering this affair was a catastrophe. It caused great damage, not only for me but Barbara and my entire family as well.

I didn't have a clue to how to get out of this mess that I had gotten myself into. I had consulted with my pastor back in Charlotte, North Carolina, as to what I should do relative to getting my life back in control. By this time, Barbara and I were both confused. Just imagine what my three children were going through. I had always protected them from outside dangers, but now, it was their father who had caused them this trauma. My pastor informed me that one of the first things that I should do was to close down the church, which was good advice because I wasn't functioning as a good example for the church, let alone my family.

It was now 1994. After having the affair with Maria, she had become pregnant with my second son. Wow! Barbara and I were trying to work on the marriage. We closed down the church and even moved back to Charlotte, hoping that we could save our marriage, but I had gotten so involved with Maria. It was very challenging, knowing that she was pregnant with my son. I felt obligated to at least be available for her.

Barbara wanted no part of keeping in contact with Maria concerning the child. The child was born on November 25, 1995. We were staying with a beautiful couple, who were members of our home church. They treated my family like their own flesh and blood. I loved this couple as well. They had welcomed my family and me with open arms, but because of my selfishness and lack of control regarding the affair with Maria, it put friction between the couple and myself.

I was back and forth from Charlotte to where Maria lived. She had moved back home with her parents. The situation was, simply put, messy. After about a year of back-and-forth, I decided it was enough. I had put Barbara through this mess long enough.

I was confused and getting other people involved in the mess as well. To stop the train wreck that I had caused, I filed for divorce, and in April 1996, in the spring, Barbara and I ended the marriage of eighteen and a half years.

I had gotten a job in Greensboro, North Carolina, doing delivery and assembling gym equipment. I used the company van to travel from Greensboro to Charlotte to see my children. I was literally all over the place. Not long after the divorce from Barbara, I decided I would *fix* the situation between Maria and me by marrying her, which only caused more problems. But in July 1996, Maria and I married in her hometown.

Throughout all the chaos that I caused through my selfishness, I never stopped seeking after God. I continued reading my Bible. I found a church that I attended regularly. Sidenote: don't think that you can live any kind of way and ask God to bless your mess. It just doesn't work that way. God is holy. He's righteous, and he does not tolerate sin ever! He is merciful, but he does not bless our mess.

I thought that marrying Maria would make things right. It did, in a sense, but it only added to the guilt that I had to deal with because of the bad decisions and choices I had made. Maria and I finally settled down into an apartment in her hometown about two hours from Charlotte. I would call or visit my older children as much as I could. Maria welcomed it, knowing that the children were suffering throughout the whole ordeal.

In June of 1997, Maria and I welcomed our second child together, a girl. I loved this little baby girl and spent much time with my son and daughter. Maria and I never really connected throughout the marriage and were at odds most of the nine years we were married.

In the summer of 1998, I decided that we would move to Charlotte in an attempt to work on our marriage and attend my home church. We moved to Charlotte, hoping that things would get better. I had a friend who was in construction and making millions of dollars. He had hired me to do various jobs for him. He made sure that I was all right financially. He even paid for the apartment that we moved into Charlotte. All through the chaos, God again used people to bless me and my family. Remember, I never gave up on God.

Maria had gotten a four-year degree and was teaching in one of the elementary schools in nearby Charlotte. I had enrolled in my church's school of ministry, hoping to someday get back into ministry. At the same time, I was responsible not only for two younger children but three older ones too. I had to withdraw from school and take on a full-time job.

It so happened that my friend who had the construction business was working on projects at the apartments where we were staying and knew the owners of the property. This gave me favor with the manager, and I was hired for a maintenance position on September 16, 1998.

We were attending my home church at the time, and my life began to get back in order. God never gave up on me because I never gave up on myself.

Oh, yeah, there were naysayers, haters. Even my biological family turned their backs on me. I never really concerned myself with people's opinions, so the church family didn't affect me much, if at all. There was much gossiping and backbiting, but hey, that was to be expected. The one sure thing about people is that they are going to talk!

After being at my home church for a few years, I wanted to start over and make a life with my new family. The company that I worked for owned apartments in several states, including Texas. I had been talking with Maria, and we decided that this would be an opportunity to get back into the ministry. In June 2000, I rented a U-Haul, packed all of our earthly possessions, and moved to Arlington, Texas.

The day that we arrived in Texas was one of the hottest days of the year. It hadn't rained in many days. I believe or recollect in eighty-seven days. One good thing—and there were several good things about moving to Texas—was I took my eldest son, Horace Jr., with me. At the time, he was really struggling. He was seventeen years old and not doing well at all with his mother, Barbara.

During the move to Texas, we were able to reestablish the father-son relationship that we enjoyed when he was a young boy. It also gave me someone I knew and could kind of hang out with. My son loved basketball, so we played a lot of it in Texas.

I had already visited Texas many times before I moved there and sort of knew what to expect. I was only transferring from Charlotte to Texas within the same company. We had our apartment awaiting us. Maria had landed a teaching position at a prominent Christian school in Arlington. My two younger children enrolled in the school as well. We had moved to Texas in hopes of starting a church, but after several attempts, I gave up and decided to join Oak Cliff Bible Fellowship located in Dallas, Texas.

CHAPTER 14

THE MOVE TO TEXAS

I've always been a student of the Word of God since becoming a Christian, and having the privilege of sitting under Pastor Tony Evans was truly a godsend. My marriage to Maria was always on shaky ground no matter how much I worked at it. The marriage was never solid. Attending church and fellowshipping with a family that we had gotten to know helped a lot, but there were always challenges. My son Horace Jr. enrolled at a local college and was able to finish school. After getting his diploma, he soon landed a job at Staples Warehouse. I was very proud of the fact that he was applying himself.

I'm old-school and believe in young men learning to take care of themselves before trying to take care of a woman. I was working in maintenance. I've always enjoyed seeing old things come to life again. Working in apartments gave me an opportunity to do just that—make things look good again.

I was good at what I did. Anything that I worked at, I always gave it my best. Moving to Texas was a whole new experience for me, and I'm sure for Maria as well. She was a military brat and could adjust to about any situation.

The company that I worked for in Charlotte had a different name in Texas and likewise was different in the way they treated their employees. After just over two years of working in the apartment industry, I resigned and took on a maintenance-supervisor job at the school/church where Maria worked and where the younger children attended. We loved this school and the faculty, staff, and students. Because there was always the fact of Maria and I breaking up my first marriage, there would never be any true peace between us. Financially, things were going well, but domestically, there was always turmoil.

Let me remind you again, this book was never written to be a religious narrative but my autobiography and an account of my life. Do what you want with the contents. I believe it will be a blessing to some and a warning to others. Sidenote: don't ever get into any meaningful relationship because of sex, especially if you want God to bless it. God cannot and will not bless mess.

I loved attending Oak Cliff. I looked forward to hearing Pastor Evans teaching on Wednesdays and Sundays. He could and still can dissect the Bible in ways that I believed will elevate your understanding of God's Word. Besides my home church in Charlotte, I could never enjoy being anywhere else other than OCBF Dallas, Texas. As a matter of fact, right before moving back to North Carolina in 2004, I had taken a maintenance position at Oak Cliff Bible Church.

In October of 2001, Maria and I welcomed our third child together. I now had three sons and four daughters, and for the record, I welcomed and love all of them. I never planned to ever get a divorce or have more children. Just like I didn't have a plan to be born, God knew. Things in life happen to all of us. We get up, shake the dust off, and move on. We can't live in yesterday!

I was now working and going to school at night. I had enrolled in a community college in Arlington. Like I've said before, I was always interested in completing and furthering my education.

The bickering and bickering between Maria and I continued all through the marriage. Neither one of us was truly happy. The beginning of the end came when one night, as I was in school, I got home and learned that Maria had packed the family van and was on her way back to her hometown in North Carolina.

I was devastated. I knew things were bad, but I never expected this. It was now February 2004, almost four years after moving to Texas. Like the times before, I had to regroup, pick myself up by the bootstraps, and keep moving. One of the attributes that I so appreciate that God put in me is resilience, the ability to bounce back quickly. Oh, thank God for his great mercy.

I couldn't just up and leave Texas. I had to withdraw from school, close out my job, rent a U-Haul, pack the furniture, etc. I soon followed Maria back to North Carolina. We rented a house there, where both of us got good jobs, but the marriage never worked out. In August 2004, Maria finally left for the last time. She quickly went to the bank, withdrew money from our account, went to the Child Support Enforcement, filed for support, and had a restraining order placed against me, claiming that I had sexually abused my baby daughter. That's how *treacherous* Maria had become after almost nine years of marriage.

I continued working on my job near the city where my children were. Because of the restraining orders and the made-up accusation of child abuse, I was arrested multiple times for just false accusations. Why am I telling my story? Because so many people, not just church people, are and do experience some of the same challenges. The devil is not partial. Give him an inch, and he will stretch it three miles. I opened the door!

I continued working on my job near Maria's hometown. This was August 2004. I had a good job, was making good money, and had several vehicles, but the *pain* of losing my (second) family was almost unbearable. There were times when I would just bow down in the floor of my apartment and cry out to God, "Father God, please help me!"

Some mornings, I could hardly think straight, but I continued crying out to God. I would read my Bible, pray, and stay in contact with a few of my friends back in Charlotte. One of them, Charles Gaskin, was a friend who stuck closer than a brother. Although over one hundred miles away, he would come to my aid wherever I needed him. It's always good and wise to have people in your life who will stand with you through thick and thin.

As long as you are willing to get out of the mess that you got yourself in, you can't pull others down. You've got to be humble enough to ask for help and willing to get up and continue living. The Bible says in Proverbs 24:16 (NKJV) that the righteous man falls seven times, and he rises up again, but the wicked stumble, are overthrown by calamity. I was determined not to quit. God had been too good to me. After all, he had given me his absolute best, his Son Jesus Christ. What more do we need?

CHAPTER 15

BACK IN CHARLOTTE

I started driving back and forth to Charlotte on the weekends to attend my home church. I knew that I needed my brothers and sisters within my church family. These are people I was familiar with, people whose shoulders I could cry on. I was hurting mentally. I needed my family!

My pastor was always willing to help me in whatever way he could. I had become suicidal. I wanted to get away. The pain, the embarrassment, the disappointment—I wanted out!

One Sunday, as I was visiting my home church, I was hurting so badly that I asked an usher to tell my pastor, who was an anointed man of God, that I needed prayer for deliverance from a spirit of suicide. The pastor called me up front, laid his hands on my forehead, took authority of the spirit that was harassing me, and I was instantly set free! That's the kind of people you need in your life when there is turmoil and chaos in your life. I will say it again, life happens to all of us.

The devil was not only using Maria to hinder my progress but also started using my supervisor at my job. After five months of fighting a good fight of faith, in December, it was on a Wednesday, the fifteenth of that month, 2004, I packed all my belongings and moved back to my hometown, the Queen City, Charlotte, North Carolina. How sweet it is!

I was so glad to be home. That night I attended church, God only knew what I had endured for nine years. I never gave up on God. Where else could I go?

When I moved back home to Charlotte, guess where I ended up. You guessed it right. I moved in with Mama.

At the time, Mom lived in a nice three-bedroom condo located on Eastway Drive in the Plaza Road area called Cityside. It was a beautiful community. Mom welcomed me because she had the room to accommodate me at the time. I always kept in contact with Mom wherever I was, either visiting or by telephone.

Once I moved in with Mom, it was like open season on my life. Mom drilled me like I was in the military. I was now in my midforties, but our parents don't seem to care how old we are. This was her chance to say whatever was on her mind. All of the things that she hadn't approved of over all those years that I was away from her *finally* surfaced. Mom even compared me to Michael Jackson. At the time, things were coming out about stuff in Michael's private life. She would say, "You and Michael Jackson has just made a mess out of your lives." Mom would be on the phone in the room next to mine, talking about me with other family members. Whether she cared if I heard her or not, it didn't matter. This was her house, and if I didn't like it, I could leave! This went on about two weeks.

I was trying hard not to disrespect my mom as much as possible, seeing that what she was saying was true, but it wasn't her business. Isn't it amazing that when you are facing hard times in your life, that's when people *seemingly* are more condemning and judgmental?

As I begin to attend my home church in Charlotte, many of the members welcomed me with open arms, some genuinely and others just being nosy! Generally, people, even those who don't know you personally, want to know where you've been. It's at these times that your *real* friends will surface. There were at least four of them who embraced me as if I was their own flesh and blood. They were Charles Gaskin, Larry (Dobie) Smith, Lawrence Price, and Pastor Robyn Gool. For this, I will always be grateful. Love you, guys!

As it happened, one of them owned some apartments and had one available at the time. He told me that the apartment needed some work done to it, but if I wanted it, it was mine. What? Whatever I needed to do to get out of my sweet mother's home, I was willing.

I didn't have a pot nor window, but God used these men and others to help me back on the road to recovery. No man is an island. There will be times in our lives when we need help from others. It's at those times when we must humble ourselves and be willing to ask for help.

I moved into the apartment around January 2005. I didn't have any furniture, but some of the men I previously mentioned gave me a kitchen table. I was given a couch, which I slept on for a while. It didn't matter. I had my own place, and for the first time in almost ten years, I was able to exhale!

I could finally get the opportunity to work on myself. We can get ourselves in situations that cost us years of time and money because of bad choices and fleshly gratifications.

As the months progressed, I was able to become more stable and where I needed to be in regard to my future. Again, let me say this: I never gave up on God. "As many as are led by the spirit of God, they are the sons of God" (Romans 8:14 KJV).

I still had to deal with some of my bad choices, and they just didn't disappear. Some of you may be asking the question, "Horace, why are you telling us all of this information? Isn't it a little or a bit much?"

I say this to you: somewhere, somebody is telling your story, and it's not *accurate*. Why not tell your own story? Write your own book. I pray that this book will inspire not only the church but those outside of the church. Start talking about your past—good, bad, or indifferent. All of us have been through things that we had no control of. It wasn't our choice, but we experienced the side effects. You may not want the world to know about your trauma, hurts, family mess, and personal failures. We've all experienced some setbacks. At least endeavor to find someone you can trust with your innermost secrets, things you wouldn't want anyone to know. Why not become vulnerable? Open up to that special person. Surely, God has put one person on this earth whom you can trust!

Only God knows all about you. The devil is not God. *He* is limited to what he knows about you. Yes, he saw you when you thought no one did. Yes, the devil heard you say that, and he will hold your past mistakes against you all of your life if you allow him to. He will even use your family, friends, and even your adult children to keep you in prison, so to speak, to your past. As Smokey the Bear says, only you can prevent forest fires!

God is a forgiving God. He doesn't hold our past against us. "As far as the east is from the west, he has removed our sins" (Psalm 103:12).

I was so grateful to Larry "Dobie" Smith that he thought enough of me to allow me to live in his apartment for such a time as that. I was away from the distractions that were keeping me from moving forward. Sometimes we can be so close to the forest that we can't enjoy the trees. I was finally enjoying some peace and quiet that I hadn't had in years.

Again, I was able to focus on myself. It was good to be back in Charlotte around familiar faces and places after being away so long. The city had grown tremendously. One thing all of us should learn is that life or the world does not stop turning when we decide to go against its gravitational pull. We bring unwanted problems into our lives when we think that our plans are better than God's plans.

I began to go through the healing process as I began to focus more on God's will for my life rather than my own. I was spending more time in fellowship with God. I was reading and studying my Bible again. It was a real pleasure to be back in my home church, seeing familiar faces, sitting under sound doctrine, hearing my pastor expound on the Bible. It was like music to my spirit. My mind was being renewed. Good things were happening.

I was attending church service every time the doors opened. I needed to be around God's people, the church. So many people, even church folk, go in the opposite direction when they encounter tests and trials. It's not the time to be isolated from others. There should be a time of restoration, not separation. There are people who genuinely love you and want what's best for you. God will bring the right people to surround you in his goodness and kindness.

I had experienced my second divorce and needed the time to heal. Divorce is a serious thing. It's like a death that has taken place, but the other person is still alive. This was my second divorce, and it was no less painful. I came to know that even then, God is the *mender* of broken hearts.

It was now the year 2005. I had been back in Charlotte several weeks. Although I was facing many challenges at the time, I had the inner strength to face whatever the challenges that presented themselves!

I started doing home improvements and selling and delivering gym equipment, so I stayed pretty much occupied. When I wasn't working or at church or visiting Mom, I was at my safe haven, my apartment. I enjoyed being in church. It was like going to therapy. Let me say this: when a man or woman has gone through separation or divorce within a month, three months, six months, or even a year—in certain circumstances, five years—this is not the time to get involved in a male or female relationship. Hurt people can sometimes, if not all the time, hurt the person they get involved with *prematurely*. It may not be their intention, but it happens.

We can look so handsome and pretty on the outside. We dress the part, sound so good, but little do people know that inside, we are torn to pieces. It takes time to heal from separation and divorce!

It's amazing how the women and men in the church can get into these premature and immature relationships without giving it a second thought, especially when children are involved. I've got to admit, I was one of the people I just mentioned. Sometimes the women seem to be so desperate that they're even asking men for a date. I'm serious! That happened to me several times. I was determined not to get myself into the trap of dating prematurely, but I did.

I wanted to be in a relationship based on friendship first. I knew that marriage was good; there are godly benefits. I had been married twice and loved being committed to one woman. After being married for twenty-seven years, albeit twice, you learn to enjoy certain attributes that come with marriage.

CHAPTER 16

MARRIAGE IS SERIOUS BUSINESS

I want to remind all of us that marriage is a very serious institution and should not be taken lightly. All through my childhood and young adult life, I saw men who had wives and carried on sexual relationships with other women. There were also married women involved in sexual relationships with other men who weren't their husbands.

I'll tell you the truth. Sex is good. Your sexual organs do not know the difference between your husband and wife, and they will perform equally to the opposite sex. Whether it's your husband or wife, your flesh doesn't have good sense. If you don't practice self-control over your body and your mental faculties, you can and often will find yourself all over the place, relative to unwanted sexual relationships. There are just as many divorces that happen within the church, if not more, than happens outside the church.

Yes, God is good; and God will forgive you for falling prey to temptation, but let's not be stupid. The Bible says in Galatians 6:7 (NKJV), "Be not deceived God is not mocked; for whatever a man or woman sows, that he will also reap." Like I have stated before, this is not intended to be a religious narrative, but let the conversation begin!

After my second divorce in January 2005, I hadn't completely gotten over the trauma that I had created through my *lack* of flesh control. I don't know how other men are built up, but I am a man. I enjoy the companionship of a woman. God created the woman and knew exactly what he was doing. He didn't make a mistake. Women, by nature are, beautiful creatures no matter how *ugly* they can act!

I have learned by experience that if you, being a real man, are going to take on this beautiful, smart, intelligent, and yes, sexy, human being, you had better start with the one who created her, God Almighty. Even if you do marry the woman of your dreams and never ever go through a divorce, you will still need God, his Son Jesus, the Holy Spirit, the angels, and the Word of God. You would have to spend time in prayer, and you may need to fast at times. Yes, counsel would help also. I'm sort of being sarcastic, but marriage is serious business.

As I close this session, let me say this: marriage is not for everybody! If you are single and never been married, there's nothing wrong with you. If you are *content* with being single, I seriously suggest that you forge a relationship with the Lord Jesus Christ. Make him your Savior and Lord. Spend time with him; fellowship with him like you would if you had a male in your life. Give him—Jesus—your all as you would that special man in your life.

Likewise, you single men, make Jesus your *everything*. He will take you places that you've never been before. You will experience the saying "Can't nobody do me like Jesus!"

Not long after my second divorce, I started seeing a lady who was a member of my home church. I hadn't really been pursuing her but had become interested in her through seeing her at church and social gatherings. I noticed that she had a son also. I was friends with her uncle, one of the brothers who had taken me in when I moved back to Charlotte. He was also there through both my divorces. He knew me quite well.

I wasn't in a hurry to start dating, so we talked on the phone mostly. At first, she indicated that she wasn't ready to enter into a relationship, so I respected that decision. I would call her periodically when I didn't see her in church just out of concern. Most of our conversations would be Sunday nights after she had put her son to bed. At first, we talked about things pertaining to church and her job. It would be late at night, but because I am not a late-night person, our conversation wouldn't be long.

I've longed to have a relationship not based on sexual, emotional imprisonment, where feelings are all over the place and you can't think right. I had my own place, and she had hers too, along with her son. At the time, she lived in another city in North Carolina.

The phone calls continued for several weeks. I knew where she worked at the time and decided to visit her on her job. I was visiting the area anyway because I shopped at the store where she was employed.

At the time, we hadn't started a serious relationship, so when I showed up at her job, she was taken by surprise. I had her paged on the company intercom. When she finally showed up, it wasn't a really good greeting. I reluctantly gave her a little hug, and she responded in kind. After a few minutes, I realized that she was busy, so I said goodbye and departed.

Later on in the day, several hours later, she called me at my home and said that she didn't appreciate me coming to her job, and she didn't like people coming unannounced. She ranted and raved for a minute or so, and I listened. Later that evening, evidently, after she had given it some thought, she called me and asked for my forgiveness. I accepted the apology, and that was the beginning of our courtship. Wow, what a beginning!

It was early January 2006. I asked her out for lunch, and she accepted the invitation. I've always believed in chivalry when it comes to a male-female relationship, so I asked her where she wanted to meet for lunch because she lived in another city about thirty minutes outside of Charlotte. I wanted to start out by respecting her decision. Our first official date was at Chili's on Highway 29.

It was important for me that we met somewhere around other people. I wanted this relationship to start out the right way. She drove her own car, and I drove mine. I believe that a *man* should have his own place to stay, drive his own car, have a job, and have some money. The woman shouldn't start out depending on the man for support right out of the gate. One thing that I admired about this woman is that she had her own apartment, her own car, a job, and her own money. She was handling her own business. She was taking care of her son. She didn't start out being needy! We started out on equal terms.

We met in the Chili's parking lot. As we arrived and got out of our vehicles, I gave her a hug, and she responded in kind. We both walked into the restaurant. As we walked up to order our lunch, I pulled out my debit card. Chivalry? This was our first time being together in public. She seemed to be enjoying our lunch and time together. This was the beginning of our relationship. I was determined to do this the right way. About an hour or so, we finished our lunch. I left a tip, and we parted ways.

As the courtship continued, I became acquainted with her son. She had raised this young man well. At the time, he was twelve years old and had good manners, something we old-school men expect from our young men.

Felicia would enroll her son Miguel into after-school programs and sign him up for basketball teams. She made sure that her son stayed active. It was at these times that she started inviting me to his basketball games. It was a real pleasure to be involved in a relationship that started out clean!

As the relationship became more serious, I asked Felicia if we should at least let her uncle and my friend Charles know that we were in a serious relationship. She let me know that she was her own woman and that it wouldn't be necessary to tell her uncle. After all, she was a *grown* woman.

After dating for a little while, I wanted our families to meet. I believe that men ought to make the woman's family feel safe about their relationship with the man they are dating. It shouldn't be hidden. After all, it is nothing to be hidden. There shouldn't be anything in the closet. All the dirty clothes ought to be brought out to be washed.

We arranged for her sisters and my family to meet at Captain Steve's on Monroe Road in Charlotte. My family liked Felicia the moment they met her. It was a good beginning to a short dating period.

Felicia and I started spending more and more time together. Each time that her son wasn't with us, I would tell her to let her son know where she was. It was important for me that he knew where his mother was and that she was safe.

Felicia and her son Miguel were close. I was the new man in her life, so I wanted it to be a smooth transition. I'm fully aware of a woman and her son's bond. I have been married before and knew somewhat about having children involved in relationships. It takes wisdom and patience on both the man and woman, especially the man.

Felicia had never been married before and hadn't had to answer to a man, so she didn't know what being *submitted* meant. This was the beginning of our test and trials. We loved being in each other's presence. But talk about independence, this woman wrote the word. Wow!

Felicia was strong-willed from first base, second, and third. It wouldn't be a home run for a while! I was determined to be a gentleman when I was with her, but only God knows how she tested everything that I was endeavoring to be.

We started dating in February 2006. We really cared for each other and had so much in common. One thing was that we both came from big families. Both of our parents were in their eighties at the time, and we both were close to our siblings.

After a few months of dating, I knew that I wanted to be with this woman. Although she was the strongest-willed woman I've ever known, I was "the man" who would help her grow into the woman she is today. I give God all of the glory!

On March 16, 2006, Felicia Michelle Gaskin became my wife. I had asked her hand in marriage a week before. She said that she would pray before giving me an answer. Shortly after that, the Lord had given her the okay!

Felicia and I had so many plans. I wanted to know what her plans were for herself and her son. I loved them and wanted the best for the both of them. We were both Christians and began to pray together, I more so because I needed God's guidance. I wanted this marriage to be successful. There have been many challenges during our almost-eighteen years of marriage, but I can truly say that God has been faithful to his promises.

My son Miguel is, as of this date, twenty-nine years old and has a career in the United States Air Force, currently a staff sergeant. Felicia finished her four-year degree in sociology and a master's degree in special education. I am back involved in ministry and, at this moment, writing my first book, and more to come. Stay tuned, and to God be all the glory.

Denise & Horace Ivey Eastway Jr. High School 1972-73

Childhood Friend Bernard "KnottyCat" Grier 1972

Childhood Best Friend Thomas "Tom" Fleming 1973

Eastway Trojans, 1973
#40, Line Backer, Horace Ivey Makes Tackle!

Homestead, 1968-2022
920 Parkwood Ave. Charlotte, North Carolina

Horace Ivey used prison 'to become a somebody'

THE NEWS HERALD Sports

By KEN GARFIELD
News Herald Sports Editor

When convicted armed robber Horace Ivey went behind bars at Western Correctional Center here in 1975, he was a 147-pound criminal full of bitterness and hate.

Today, nearly two years after being released from the youthful offender prison, he is "Mr. Charlotte." A bodybuilder of spreading fame, Ivey is 196 pounds of rippling muscle.

But more than that, Ivey, now 20, has used bodybuilding, weightlifting and his experience in prison to turn his life and his future around.

He recently drove from his home in Charlotte to the high-rise prison where he was an inmate to visit prison workers who started him on the road to being muscle-bound.

"When I first went in," Ivey recalled, "I wasn't too interested in anything except getting out. Me and coach Johnson (recreation worker Harold Johnson) got to be pretty good friends. He got me into weight training.

"I always told him I was going to be somebody," Ivey said.

Ivey, who is 5 feet 10 inches tall, started out bench pressing 140 pounds. Working out two hours a day, every day, in the hallway that serves as the prison's weight room, he strained and struggled. Slowly, he worked his way up to heavier weights.

With Johnson's help, Ivey's physique began to improve, and he eventually lifted weights near the 400-pound mark.

"Just working out, being around weights, got my mind off being in here," Ivey explained on his return visit to the prison.

By the time his prison sentence expired in late 1977 and he headed back to his Charlotte home, Ivey was in great shape, and he was committed to bodybuilding.

He hooked up with Lance Packing Company, a Charlotte-based industry which supports bodybuilders. Now, with Lance's financial backing and already holding the "Mr. Charlotte" title, he's going to compete for the "Mr. America" crown next month in New York City.

Ivey's former coach, who probably sees more failures than successes inside the prison, is thrilled at his ex-pupil's success. Johnson now has 150 prisoners working with weights.

"The kids have heard me talk so much about Horace," Johnson says. "I tell them it can work if they have the determination. Horace is someone all our boys try to shoot for."

Ivey doesn't like to talk about the armed robbery that sent him to prison. He's much more at ease talking about his wife ("She pushes me out of the house to go train") and his infant daughter, both of whom accompany him to bodybuilding competitions.

After a brief workout in the prison weight room, where guards watched in awe, Ivey headed to the upper floors to visit prisoners who live in what he called "my old domain."

"Thank God," Ivey said quietly as he rode up in the prison elevator, "this was the first time I was in trouble and I was able to take advantage of it.

"Now I just want to show the public that someone in here can make something of himself."

Article of Me, Visiting the Highrise in Morganton, North Carolina

A photo of me, just showing off!
Circa 1979

Family Portrait, June 2, 2018
Vivian, Denise "NeNe", Lloyd, Deborah, Jimmy,
Horace, Linda, and Thelma "Mama"

ABOUT THE AUTHOR

Horace was born on June 1, 1958, in Charlotte, North Carolina. He is the fifth of eight children. He enjoyed being around his brothers, sisters, and cousins, whom he loved dearly. Although the family did not have much in terms of material things, the love of one another filled the void. He attended the Charlotte Mecklenburg Public School System, where he often said that lunch and physical education were his favorite subjects.

Horace enjoys various hobbies, such as reading about history, bodybuilding, cross-country walking, fishing, boating, sitting on the beach for hours, climbing the Blue Ridge Mountains, and never meeting a stranger.

Horace's greatest accomplishment was being awarded his General Education Diploma (GED) in 1976, two years ahead of his little sister Nene. A second accomplishment was in 1979, competing in the WBBG Mr. America, placing third in the middle-class competition.

He has eight children, one of whom is his stepson, whom he loves as if he were his own flesh and blood. He has ten grandchildren and four great-grandchildren. He has been married for eighteen years to the love his life, Felicia Gaskin-Ivey.

Horace often talks about being a baby boomer and has an old-school mentality. He says, "Do what you say that you are going to do and give it your all! Failure is not an option!" If you seem to fail, get back up again. "For a righteous man may fall seven times and rise again" (Proverbs 24:16 NKJV).